CONCISE
LINCOLN
LIBRARY

—

EDITED BY RICHARD W. ETULAIN,
SARA VAUGHN GABBARD, AND
SYLVIA FRANK RODRIGUE

JOHN F. MARSZALEK

Lincoln and the Military

Southern Illinois University Press
Carbondale

Printed in the United States of America

17 16 15 14 4 3 2 1

The Concise Lincoln Library has been made possible in part through a generous donation by the Leland E. and LaRita R. Boren Trust.

Library of Congress Cataloging-in-Publication Data
Marszalek, John F., 1939–
Lincoln and the military / John F. Marszalek.
pages cm. — (Concise Lincoln library)
Includes bibliographical references and index.
ISBN 978-0-8093-3361-5 (cloth : alk. paper)
ISBN 0-8093-3361-9 (cloth : alk. paper)
ISBN 978-0-8093-3362-2 (ebook)
ISBN 0-8093-3362-7 (ebook)
1. Lincoln, Abraham, 1809–1865—Military leadership. 2. United States—History—Civil War, 1861–1865—Campaigns. 3. Civil-military relations—United States—History—19th century. I. Title.
E457.2.M364 2014
973.7092—dc23 2014008176

Printed on recycled paper. ♲
The paper used in this publication meets the minimum requirements of American National Standard for Information Sciences—Permanence of Paper for Printed Library Materials, ANSI Z39.48-1992. ∞

For the Lincoln Forum

CONTENTS

PREFACE

Books have been written on just about every aspect of Abraham Lincoln's life and career. The American public knows more about him than it does about any other U.S. president, although too much of this knowledge is inaccurate or exaggerated fable. Next to Lincoln's childhood, sense of humor, and assassination, his role as military leader of the Union war effort seems to particularly interest the reading public.

Of the many books written on this topic, two stand out in importance. In 1952, T. Harry Williams, the late professor of history at Louisiana State University, wrote his classic *Lincoln and His Generals*, describing in detail Lincoln's Civil War military activities. In 2008, James M. McPherson, professor emeritus of history at Princeton University, wrote *Tried by War: Abraham Lincoln as Commander in Chief.* This book shared the Lincoln Prize for 2009 with *Lincoln and His Admirals*, by the U.S. Naval Academy's retired professor Craig Symonds. These books are thoroughly researched and beautifully written, and they provide the reader with important insights into Lincoln's military activities.

Other important volumes have helped the public learn about Lincoln's role in the war. Kenneth P. Williams's five-volume *Lincoln Finds a General: A Military Study of the Civil War* (1949–59) remains the most detailed study of this topic. Biographies of the Civil War's leading generals and monographs concerning individual battles and campaigns also throw a light on Lincoln, as do Civil War textbooks and studies of American warfare.

The best primary source for the study of this topic is *The Collected Works of Abraham Lincoln*, edited by Roy P. Basler, published in ten volumes plus index (1953–55, 1974, 1990). This work presents letters and speeches made by Lincoln and is a gold mine of information on his war activity. A modern editorial project called *The Papers of Abraham Lincoln*, led by Daniel W. Stowell, is one of the most exciting historical undertakings of our time. Its purpose is to find and publish all documents that Abraham Lincoln wrote or received during his lifetime (1809–65). A recent compilation of Lincoln's war words, *Lincoln on War* (2011), edited by Harold Holzer, is an excellent source for a quick study of the topic.

This book, *Lincoln and the Military*, presents a brief account of his role as a military leader, an important topic in both the life of Abraham Lincoln and the history of the nation. It is based primarily on his own words. It demonstrates that this man made mistakes but grew as a military leader. His determination, sense of humor, analytical ability, quickness to learn important information, and humility toward those he encountered helped him become the success that he was.

Before many others did, Lincoln recognized the connection between union and liberty, and that insight served as a lodestar throughout his military efforts. Early in the war, he realized that the destruction of slavery was necessary for the Union to be preserved or, to put it another way, that the Union war effort could be successful only if it attacked the institution of slavery. Lincoln knew too that he had to use the war powers the Constitution provided the president in order for him to be a successful war leader. Abraham Lincoln saved the Union; he destroyed slavery; he used his constitutionally granted powers widely; and in doing these things, he became the most successful war president in American history.

One facet of Lincoln's leadership that cannot be considered in detail in a volume of this size is how he embraced the technological innovation that occurred during the Civil War and had an enormous influence on the way the war was fought. The four years of internal conflict both sped up innovation in some fields and slowed it down in others. Four years is not a very long period of time, yet the nation that went into war in 1861 emerged as a different entity in 1865. In truth, however, much of this technological change had already begun in the 1850s, before the war's inception.

Clearly, the technological change that had the greatest impact on the war was the movement from the smoothbore musket to the minié ball–loaded rifle. This increased the length and width of the battlefield from one hundred to eight hundred yards, and the cylindrical lead minié balls with their hollow bases caused horrendous wounds when they hit the human body. Repeating rifles also became more common, thanks to inventors like Christopher Spencer and B. Tyler Henry. Richard J. Gatling created the multiple-barrel machine gun, but the Gatling gun was not generally used in warfare until later in the century. Artillery changed, too, in the form of the rifled cannon and the better targeting of the long used and more numerous smoothbore.

Other inventions that affected the fighting of the war included revolving pistols, land and naval mines (torpedoes), grenades, and flame throwers. Such weaponry changed warfare from mass attacks across a battlefield and advancing in elbow-to-elbow formations to trench warfare and advancing in rushes.

The navies also experienced amazing changes as the war progressed. Most importantly, the traditional wooden sailing ships gave way to steam-powered ironclads, which in later years became all-metal vessels. The famous *Monitor* was like no ship sailors had ever seen before as it fought its battle with the Confederate *Merrimack*. The navies tried submarines too, but these were never strategically significant. Still, a Confederate submarine called the *Huntley* sank a Union blockader, *Housatonic*, in Charleston Harbor. Later progress in submarine technology resulted in the United States entering World War I over its belief that the underwater vessel was being used illegally.

Improvements in already existing technology not only affected the fighting of the war but also made an impression on civilian society. The railroad came into existence in the United States in the 1830s, and by the 1850s, it was an integral part of American life. During the Civil War, it played a major role in moving troops and keeping them supplied. Trains ran only about twenty-five miles per hour, but they were still faster than any other means of transportation. The fact that the Federals had more track, and generally of the same gauge, gave the North a major advantage over the Confederates, who had less track and a variety of gauges. Battles were fought over such railroad sites as Manassas Junction, Corinth, Atlanta, and Chattanooga. The unification of all the Northern railroads into the U.S. Military Railroad System gave the North a real advantage in these and other battles.

Especially important to the war and society was the telegraph, which Samuel F. B. Morse invented in 1844. This prewar instrument made it possible for Civil War generals to communicate over the length and breadth of the battlefield, giving them a tactical and strategic flexibility commanders had never had before. Armies even strung telegraph wire behind them as they advanced on the enemy, thus constantly expanding the telegraph's range.

The telegraph also allowed newspapers to report quickly to the home front about conditions on the battlefield. To gather the news, the press sent correspondents to the front, and these reporters often sent home information that generals and political officials did not want to see publicized. Newspapers thus let their readers know the good and the bad about politicians and military leaders, although they sometimes simply made up stories about them. In any case, they played a major role in forming public opinion, as did the expansion of the Associated Press during the war. The innovation-driven drop in newspaper prices also allowed for the news to be spread more widely.

Popular magazines like *Harper's Weekly* and *Frank Leslie's Illustrated Newspaper* employed artists to draw pictures of events on the battlefield and images of leading war politicians and military officers. For the first time in American history, people could see what most of the leaders and the distant battlefields looked like.

Hot air and hydrogen balloons were prewar innovations that showed enormous promise. Rising high above the battlefield, whether floating in the atmosphere or remaining in one key spot tethered to the ground, those aloft in these balloons could even send telegraphic messages telling commanders what the enemy was up to. Such information had never been available on battlefields before. Yet internal conflict among balloonists and lack of interest among commanders soon grounded these air machines.

On the battlefield and in society, tin cans grew into general use, allowing both soldiers and civilians to stock food for later use. These containers held bland food, but they were significant in keeping millions of people fed. The use of salted meat grew in importance for the same reason.

Treatment of the wounded on the battlefield also improved with the greater use of chloroform. Still, medical science was hardly close to modern because the germ theory was not yet recognized. The general amputation of limbs as a method of saving a wounded man's life still made medical care in the armies horrendous, but improvement in prosthetic limbs helped the amputees. Transportation of the wounded was systemized, and huge hospitals were established behind the lines, along with field hospitals near the battlefield. Even today, the ambulance system of the Civil War remains the model for battlefield treatment of soldiers.

Abraham Lincoln, the only president ever to have acquired a patent (for a device that lifted ships over shoals), was enthralled with these innovations, and he was willing to test any invention that he hoped might shorten the war. Unfortunately, the army bureaucracy was mired in the past and was unfriendly toward any modern innovations. This attitude stymied military progress.

The exact impact on the Civil War of all such innovations is not easily delineated. The contemporary *Scientific American* magazine published information on the latest technology, demonstrating the changes at work in society and on the battlefield. A 1956 book by Robert V. Bruce titled *Lincoln and the Tools of War* remains the best compilation of Lincoln's activities in this sphere.

Describing all the innovations that helped bring about a change in warfare during this period and were steps in the evolution to modern war, however, are beyond the scope of this book. For the purposes of this volume, suffice it to say that Abraham Lincoln attempted to employ whatever technology he could. He used the telegraph, the railroad, and the press, and he did not shy away from any killing instrument, no matter its potential horror. In the end, however, it was not innovation that directed his leadership but more intangible matters, which this book strives to explain.

This book stands on the shoulders of the many other publications that preceded it. However, it was only when I met Frank J. Williams and Harold Holzer at a Civil War conference in Florida in 1997 that I, a William T. Sherman biographer, came more completely into the world of Abraham Lincoln. I became a member of the board of advisors of the Lincoln Forum, the organization that these two leading Lincoln scholars founded and still lead. More than one historian has benefited from the expertise and encouragement of these two men. The fact that I am now the executive director of the Ulysses S. Grant Association's Ulysses S. Grant Presidential Library at Mississippi State University can be traced back to the Lincoln Forum.

It was at the annual forum meetings in Gettysburg that my wife, Jeanne, and I first came to know Frank and Virginia Williams, Harold and Edith Holzer, Craig and Marylou Symonds, Russ Weidman (and the departed Budge), Edna Greene Medford, George Buss, Tom Horrocks, Don McCue, Linda Wheeler, Joe Fornieri, Everett and Antigone Ladd, Jim Santagata, Mike Marlow, Dick Crews, Mel Maurer, Betty Anselmo, Henry Ballone, Bill Spears, Marty and Jane Waligorski, Ken Childs, Malcolm Garber, and so many other people, some noted historians, others Lincoln enthusiasts. I wish I could mention everyone, because I learned so much from my fellow members of the Lincoln Forum. I am happy to dedicate this book to them all.

Moreover, this entire Concise Lincoln Library would not be possible without its outstanding editors, Richard W. Etulain, Sara Vaughn Gabbard, and Sylvia Frank Rodrigue, and the staff of Southern Illinois University Press, especially Rodrigue, who also serves as its talented acquisitions editor.

I also benefited from the close reading of this manuscript by the three editors, outstanding historians Frank J. Williams and Timothy B. Smith, and an anonymous reader. My assistant at the Ulysses S. Grant Presidential Library, Meg Henderson, helped throughout the process of completing this manuscript.

Jeanne remains the love of my life and has the sharpest eye for wayward facts and prose.

LINCOLN AND THE MILITARY

CHAPTER ONE

"NO COMMANDER EVER STARTED WITH A HEAVIER HANDICAP"

The president's role as commander in chief of the U.S. military has its official origin in the Constitution. When the Founding Fathers composed this document in 1787, they indicated that the president held "executive power" and was "Commander in Chief of the Army and Navy of the United States, and of the Militia of the several States, when called into the actual Service of the United States." Fresh from the Revolutionary War, the delegates wanted to make sure that the new nation could react swiftly and surely to any military threat, so they supported the idea of the president holding significant military power. A few delegates disagreed. Elbridge Gerry saw such executive military power as a threat to domestic tranquility and worried that a "Despot" might arise who "may draw out his dragoons to suppress the murmurs of the few."[1]

Even though this matter has been debated and interpreted in many ways, presidential powers have expanded over the years. The U.S. Congress and Supreme Court have attempted to hold these powers down, but they have only grown greater. In a phrase, the president determines the use of the military.[2]

It is not all that clear-cut in the Constitution. Where the Founding Fathers enumerated the powers of Congress, they inserted statements indicating that it had military authority too: "The Congress shall have Power . . . To declare War . . . ; To raise and support Armies . . . ; To provide and maintain a Navy; To make Rules for the Government and Regulation of the land and naval Forces; To provide for calling forth the Militia to execute the Laws of the Union, suppress Insurrections and repel Invasions; [and] To provide for organizing, arming, and disciplining, the Militia, and for governing such Part of them as may be employed in the Service of the United States."[3]

In the twenty-first century, Americans still debate the division of such powers, but presidential authority remains superior and definitive. Congress does have the power to declare war, but since the 1940s, this simply has not happened. The president has decided where to send troops into combat without congressional declaration that a state of war existed. Congressional withholding of appropriations for such combat would certainly be constitutional, but such action is not politically possible. The threat of electoral repercussions for refusing to support the troops in combat is too great for Congress even to consider. Thus the president is able to act unilaterally, regardless of public opinion or congressional complaint.

It was during the nineteenth century that presidential military power increased. James Madison was president during the War of 1812, but his role in the war was minimal. The Mexican War of the 1840s saw civic conflict between political parties and between President James K. Polk and Congress. As a later historian has written, however, Polk "demonstrated clearly that a civilian Commander in Chief could effectively direct and control a major war effort; he could in short run a war."[4]

Consequently, when the Civil War erupted in the 1860s during the presidency of Abraham Lincoln, the chief executive's military power had a constitutional basis, which had experienced effective expansion under Polk during the Mexican War. Lincoln had been a member of Congress during that war, and as an intelligent observer, he saw clearly what was going on. He honored the Constitution, but he revered the Declaration of Independence even more. He also knew the laws of war, and he brought with him a lifetime of experiences, including a brief stint in the militia. These experiences, along with his sharp intellect, ability to learn, abundant political skills, common sense, and humility, together with his view of the Constitution—that is, to do "things within a constitutional framework"[5]—determined the success of his military activities during the Civil War.

Lincoln ultimately based his war-making powers on his insistence that no state had a constitutional right to secede from the Union. He maintained that it was the Union that had created the states, not vice versa, and this had been done with the promulgation of the Declaration of Independence.[6] His duty as president was to preserve that Union, and his power to accomplish that was constitutional. The Confederacy argued that the sovereignty of the states had existed before that of the Union. When the states joined the Union, they still kept their basic sovereignty. And because they had joined the Union by convention, they could leave it by the same device. Lincoln disagreed, and the war came.

Abraham Lincoln was born in 1809 and spent his early life on the rough-and-tumble frontier of Kentucky, Indiana, and Illinois. He was no stranger to violence—of all kinds. He wrestled with the strong man in his village, and he pursued all the rowdy pastimes that young men of that period craved. In 1832, as a poor resident of New Salem, Illinois, and a member of the ill-trained 31st Regiment of the Illinois Militia, he and some other economically challenged young men volunteered for thirty days' service in the Black Hawk War. He did not want to become a military leader, but he was elected captain anyway, as his friends were determined to put him in charge.

Lincoln had no military experience when he went into this war, and he demonstrated it. According to one story, although its veracity has been debated, he became stymied when his marching militia unit encountered a fence in its way. Not knowing the command to get his unit through a break in the obstruction, he allegedly stopped his men, dismissed them, and told them to re-form on the far side of the fence. Another time, he disobeyed a standing order not to fire a weapon near camp and was arrested for a day. On yet another occasion, when his men stole some wine and whiskey and were unable to march the next day, he was arrested and forced to wear the badge of officerly incompetence, a large wooden sword.[7]

Despite his obvious lack of military knowledge and such martial blunders, Lincoln still gained the respect of his men by a display of courage that he repeated under different conditions in later years. This time, an old Indian, carrying a pass, arrived at the camp of Lincoln's unit. Militia members immediately tried to pounce on the poor man, threatening to kill him because he was the enemy. Lincoln refused to allow this to occur and placed himself between his men and the Native American. "The Indian is a damned spy," the soldiers shouted. Lincoln refused to budge. "This is cowardly on your part, Lincoln," the men accused. Lincoln forcefully responded, "If any man thinks I am a coward let him test it." No one did.[8]

In fact, Lincoln and his militia never fought any Indians. They did become cold, wet, and hungry before their thirty days were up, however, and they experienced many of the fears every soldier does. When the New Salem unit broke up and went home, Lincoln volunteered to stay on as a private with another unit, but again he saw no combat.

Lincoln later joked about it all on the floor of the U.S. House of Representatives. "By the way, Mr. Speaker, did you know I am a military Hero? Yes sir; in the days of the Black Hawk War, I fought, bled, and came away. . . . I had a good many bloody struggles with the mosquitoes; and, although I never fainted from loss of blood, I can truly say I was often very hungry."[9]

Lincoln was fiercely proud of his military service, even though he believed that it had not amounted to much. In reality, he "had learned the rudiments of soldiering." He knew what it was like to be a common soldier who never lost his independent spirit. He was thrilled that his townsmen had expressed enough confidence in him to choose him as their officer, which he said was "a success which gave me more pleasure than any I have had since." Clearly, Lincoln's less-than-exacting career as a soldier made him proud and provided him with some military insight. Unlike some other individuals of that period, however, he never developed hubris about supposed military experience.[10]

Upon his return to New Salem, Lincoln pursued an interest that would come to dominate his life: politics. He ran for the state legislature from his home county. Four seats were up for election that year, but Lincoln finished eighth out of thirteen candidates. Significantly, however, he took 277 out of the 300 votes cast in New Salem. He had clearly impressed his friends and neighbors with his service in the Indian war.[11]

When a more famous Indian fighter became the favorite in the 1840 presidential campaign, Lincoln strongly supported the hero of Tippecanoe, Whig William Henry Harrison. Being Whigs themselves, Lincoln and several friends anonymously put together a circular of support for Harrison, titling it *The Old Soldier*. Word got out quickly, however, that they were the ones behind the publication. They responded with another flier, filling it with military phrases to support Harrison's cause. All "old soldiers," it said, must "form into 'battle array'" to fight "an organized army of office-holders [that] is now fitting out an expedition against your old commander. They are coming armed—not with bristling steel, because that bedazzles their eyes—not with powder and balls, because the smell of sulphur offends their nostrils, but with falsehood, slander, and detraction, upon the characters of yourselves and your chieftain, established in the hard and bloody conflicts with your country's invading enemies."[12]

Later, Lincoln won a seat in the U.S. House of Representatives, but only when the Mexican War was practically over. He opposed the conflict as unjust and proposed a resolution that would haunt him for the rest of his political life. On December 22, 1847, he introduced what came to be called the "Spot Resolutions." He pointed out that President James K. Polk had insisted in several messages to Congress that Mexico had "invaded *our territory*, and shed the blood of our fellow *citizens on our own soil*." Lincoln demanded that Polk prove to Congress that "the spot of soil on which the blood of our *citizens* was shed" was indeed part of American territory.[13]

The rival Democrats were not impressed. They employed an argument that would be repeated often in the future, claiming that Lincoln and the Whigs were not supporting the troops. Conversely, Lincoln and his party said that by voting to supply the troops, they were really supporting them. Lincoln learned quickly that an antiwar position was politically difficult to maintain. In a letter to a Baptist minister who supported Polk and the war, Lincoln held his ground, however. He reminded the parson of what he considered as U.S. aggression against the Mexicans and the destruction of their crops. "Is the precept 'Whatsoever ye would that men should do to you, do ye even so to them' obsolete?—of no force?—of no application?"[14]

Constantly refining his position, Lincoln composed one of those private fragments in March that he frequently wrote when he was trying to organize his thoughts. This time he surmised how possible presidential candidate Zachary Taylor should respond to the criticisms against his Whig Party. Taylor should say, Lincoln insisted, "As to the Mexican war, I still think the defensive line policy the best to terminate it." In the forthcoming treaty of peace, Lincoln believed Taylor should oppose adding any territory that would "enlarge and agrivate [*sic*] the distracting question of slavery." "Finally, were I president," Lincoln wanted Taylor to say, "I should desire the legislation of the country to rest with Congress, uninfluenced by the executive in it's [*sic*] origin or progress, and undisturbed by the veto unless in very special and clear cases."[15]

In 1848, after the Whigs nominated Zachary Taylor, the Democrats mocked them for opposing the war yet nominating a general as their candidate. In a July 27 speech to the U.S. House, Lincoln insisted that Whigs, like Democrats, had fought and died in the Mexican War, but the Democrats just could not understand the subtlety of the Whig position. "The distinction between the cause of the *President* in beginning the war, and the cause of the *country* after it was begun, is a distinction which you cannot perceive," Lincoln told the Democrats. There were plenty of Whigs who "underwent extraordinary perils and hardships" in fighting the war, yet they believed "that the war was unnecessarily and unconstitutionally commenced by the President." As a soldier, Taylor knew his task was not to question the war, Lincoln said, but to "bring it to a speedy and honorable termination, by the most vigorous and energetic operations."[16]

The post–Mexican War period saw no further foreign war, but events during these years continued to demonstrate the difficulties of the American military system. The president was indeed the commander in chief, but in the public eye, the military consisted of the army and navy, the secretaries of war and the navy, a commanding general of the land forces, and officers of the small American fleet. The presidents and Congress in the 1850s spent more time on debates over slavery in the territories than on questions of military authority. And a ludicrous military dispute exploded.

Jefferson Davis was the secretary of war in the administration of Franklin Pierce (1853–1857), and the commanding general was Winfield Scott. The debate over who had authority over whom resulted in what seemed to be an unending struggle between the two military leaders. Each man insisted that he had ultimate control over the army. The disagreement soon became personal. Davis wrote to Scott, "Your petulance, characteristic egotism and recklessness of accusation have imposed on me the task of unveiling some of your deformities," among them "querulousness, insubordination, greed of lucre and want of truth." Not to be outdone, Scott responded, "My silence, under the new provocation, has been the result, first of pity, and next forgetfulness. Compassion is always due to an enraged imbecile."[17] Personality replaced policy, and Lincoln must have wondered what this meant.

In 1858, when Lincoln was challenging Stephen A. Douglas for the Illinois U.S. Senate seat, his antiwar stance during the Mexican War came back to haunt him again. Potential opponents insisted that Lincoln not only had been opposed to the war but also had voted against providing the troops with needed supplies. He had to defend himself to Joseph Medill, one of the copublishers of the critical *Chicago Tribune*, and during the debates with Douglas, Lincoln had to protest again. In Pekin, Illinois, he denounced the accusation that he had "helped starve his brothers and friends in the Mexican War by voting against the bills appropriating to them money, provisions, and medical attendance." Even when he ran for president in 1860, opponents still accused him of voting against supplying troops during the Mexican War, and once again he had to protest his innocence.[18]

When Abraham Lincoln was elected president of the United States in 1860, therefore, his reputation and rhetoric were antiwar. He insisted that he knew what the Constitution said and would govern under it. Yet he became a president who proved unafraid to stretch the document to preserve the Union and destroy slavery. The nation had elected a militarily forthright chief executive, who had limited military experience and little knowledge about military tactics and strategy when the Southern states seceded and the war began.

Lincoln realized that his enemy was formidable. The Southern states, united under the name Confederate States of America, possessed an enormous amount of territory, from the Atlantic Ocean west across the Appalachian Mountains, past the Mississippi River, and north of the Gulf of Mexico toward the Ohio River. The Confederacy had a tradition of military schools and militias, and a large number of West Point graduates lived within its borders. Its army eventually approached one million men. The Confederacy's cotton culture produced wealth and had a longtime connection to Europe, particularly England. Its chattel labor worked in the fields, as well as the factories and mines, freeing white men for military service. The Confederacy also had a particularly important military advantage. All it had to do was survive and it would win its independence.

Lincoln's United States had the more difficult task. It had a larger population than its opponent, with a broader economic base, but the necessity of having to conquer in order to win negated such advantages. The United States had to go on the offensive and win quickly and significantly in order to maintain its optimism and deflate the confidence of its opponents. On paper, the United States looked invincible, but in reality, either side had a chance of winning or losing. To preserve the Union would require effective leadership within the framework of the Constitution. It was up to Abraham Lincoln to provide that leadership, and his past indicated that he had limitations. He had been antiwar during the nation's last war and opposed to the concept of a strong military president.

His adversary demonstrated more promise. Jefferson Davis was a West Point graduate, a hero of the Mexican War, and one of the nation's great secretaries of war. Yet there is common agreement among historians that Lincoln became the superior presidential military strategist. The great military thinker Carl von Clausewitz perhaps explained it best. Military experience was not the "principal requirement." Of greater importance were "a remarkable, superior mind and strength of character." Lincoln started off with major military weaknesses, but his growth as a leader and his ability to overcome enormous difficulties were decisive. Yet, as a British general wrote in the 1960s, "no commander ever started with a heavier handicap."[19]

CHAPTER TWO

"WHY DON'T THEY COME!"

In the 1860 election, Abraham Lincoln was the candidate of the neophyte Republican Party, and his party's only unifying principle was opposition to slavery in the territories. The Democratic Party split and ran Southern and Northern candidates, while a fourth party ran a candidate on the platform of compromise to prevent secession. Lincoln won the majority of the electoral vote but gained only about 40 percent of the popular vote. He was hardly a landslide winner.

After his victory in the election that November, Lincoln had to face the December 20, 1860, to February 1, 1861, secession of South Carolina, Mississippi, Florida, Alabama, Georgia, Louisiana, and Texas. He worried that his opponents would ensure that no quorum would be present in Congress to count the electoral votes officially naming him president, but he was more concerned about how to handle the secession crisis. As he traveled from his home in Springfield, Illinois, to the nation's capital for his inauguration, he stopped along the way and expressed his evolving ideas in speeches to the populace. In Indianapolis on February 11, for example, Lincoln wrestled with warnings from the public and its leaders against using "coercion" or "invasion" against the seceded states. If he sent an army into South Carolina without the people's permission, he admitted, this would be an invasion. However, "if the Government . . . simply insists upon holding its own forts, or retaking those forts which belong to it," then Lincoln did not see that as aggression. He insisted, though, that he had made no decision and was only "giving something for [listeners] to reflect upon." When he reached Philadelphia on George Washington's birthday, Lincoln told his expectant audience at Independence (Constitution) Hall that "there will be no blood shed unless it is forced upon the Government." Lincoln did not want to go to war.[1]

Recognizing his own military shortcomings, Lincoln looked to his army leaders to help guide his reaction to any crisis that might develop. He felt fortunate to have as his commanding general one of the true military heroes of the nineteenth century, Winfield Scott. The six-foot, five-inch Scott had fought brilliantly in the War of 1812 and the Mexican War. By 1861, however, he was seventy-five years old, with all the ailments of the aged. He was unable to provide his president with the military leadership the chief executive needed and wanted. Scott had not even planned for the war that was clearly on the horizon. His famous Anaconda Plan was really a knee-jerk reaction to an absurd suggestion from a junior officer named George B. McClellan to conduct an over-the-mountains campaign to capture Richmond and thus win the war in one swift blow.

As Scott had not done any prior planning, his reaction to McClellan was hardly conclusive. The commanding general said he wanted to prepare Federal forces well and then move them down the Mississippi River, while simultaneously instituting a blockade of the Confederacy. Then, like a giant snake, Union forces would squeeze the Confederacy out of existence without having to go on the offensive. This so-called Anaconda Plan had one major defect, which Scott failed to see. Surrounding the Confederacy and then waiting for it to succumb would take time and give it the chance of outlasting the United States and thus winning the war.[2]

Yet Scott was a military expert and more than willing to advise Lincoln, even before the November election and the advent of secession. At that time, he sent the candidate a memorandum explaining his perceptions of what was looming on the horizon, warning of the "imminent danger of a disruption of the Union by the secession of one or more southern states." He believed that Lincoln had to dampen the furor surrounding the debate over slavery in the territories by pointing out that it was "unprofitable" for slavery to exist in the western plains. "A policy of moderation and firmness for the next twelve months would perhaps prevent secession," Scott surmised.[3]

Lincoln kept in regular touch with Scott and treated the commanding general with the utmost respect, but he still let it be known who was in charge. He insisted that if President James Buchanan should order the surrender of any federal forts before Lincoln's March 1861 inauguration, "the General must retake them afterwards." Lincoln wanted Scott "to be as well prepared as he [could] to either *hold*, or *retake*, the forts, as the case may require." Even before he took office, therefore, Lincoln had made essential military decisions. He also told Scott that he expected regular reports from him. These would not only help educate Lincoln in the ways of the military but also demonstrate who was in charge.[4]

Additionally, Lincoln hoped for advice from outgoing president James Buchanan, but he was appalled when "Old Buck" merely gave him information about the kitchen and pantry, especially noting that "the water of the right-hand well at the White House [was] better than that at the left." Buchanan was biding his time until his term of office was over, and he would not help Lincoln in any way.[5]

Lincoln decided that he had to build a cabinet that represented all elements of the new Republican Party. He wanted Scott and another ancient soldier, John E. Wool, to be his chief military advisors, but he settled on Simon Cameron, a Pennsylvania boss, to be his secretary of war.[6]

Meanwhile, Fort Sumter became the symbol for the entire secession disagreement, and Lincoln had to solve this problem before he could deal with anything else. Would war break out if the South tried to take Sumter or if the North tried to preserve its hold over it? Buchanan had told Congress that secession was illegal but that the president could not prevent it. Yet he had tried to resupply and reinforce Major Robert Anderson and his garrison of about eighty men at this fort in Charleston Harbor, South Carolina. He had sent the *Star of the West* with supplies and two hundred soldiers to Charleston, but on January 9, 1861, the Confederates had fired on this ship and driven it off. Anderson and his men had to hold on without outside help, and Anderson was determined to do so.[7]

Once Lincoln's inauguration was over in early March, he had to do something about Fort Sumter. On March 9, Lincoln asked Commanding General Winfield Scott to update him on the military situation there. The old soldier responded that Anderson and his troops might be able to hold out for a month or so longer, but he could not resupply them in that short a time. It would take at least eight months and "a fleet of war vessels & transports, 5,000 additional regular troops & 20,000 volunteers." A week later Lincoln asked his cabinet about the wisdom of resupply, and he received similarly pessimistic answers. Most of the cabinet members insisted that Lincoln should do nothing that might provoke a war.[8]

Lincoln wondered what he could or should do. Congress asked him to provide copies of the letters that Fort Sumter commander Robert Anderson had sent to Washington, but Lincoln politely refused. He wanted to keep things close to his own vest. On April 1, facing another political demand, he answered a letter from William Henry Seward in which the secretary of state criticized Lincoln's lack of "policy either domestic or foreign" and insisted that the Lincoln administration defend Fort Pickens in Florida and let Fort Sumter fall. This would take attention away from the South Carolina fort and lessen the present crisis there, he said. Seward even volunteered to take control of these matters while Lincoln stood in the background. Lincoln quickly put Seward in his place and continued trying to devise a solution to the problems facing him.[9]

On April 6, Lincoln made his decision. He sent a State Department clerk to the governor of South Carolina and told him that a resupply expedition, but no additional troops, would soon be reaching Charleston. No hostile action would occur unless the Confederacy began it, Lincoln asserted. Now it was Confederate president Jefferson Davis's turn to respond to Lincoln's decision. He had to act or the Confederacy would lose the momentum of secession. At four thirty in the morning on April 12, 1861, Confederate artillery opened fire on Robert Anderson and the Union soldiers in Fort Sumter. No Federal was hurt, but Anderson and his small unit had to surrender on April 14.[10]

Did Lincoln cleverly maneuver the South into firing the first shot, as some later historians have charged? It does not seem so.

During the tense period since Lincoln and Davis had taken office, the Confederate president had been hoping that the Federals would make the first attack. On April 3, 1861, Davis had even written to his good friend Braxton Bragg, then commanding troops ready to attack Union-held Fort Pickens in Florida, that he hoped the Confederates could maneuver the Federals into firing the first shot at Pickens. Before Bragg could act, however, it became clear that forcing the Federals to fire first would require a potentially problematic frontal attack. Davis feared a disaster, so he turned his attention back to Fort Sumter. As Professor Grady McWhiney wrote, "Thus war came at Fort Sumter only because the Confederates were neither subtle enough nor strong enough to begin it at Fort Pickens."[11] Lincoln won, but he lost too. The Confederates took the blame for starting a war that Lincoln did not want to see happen.

Lincoln wasted no time in responding, however. Three days after Fort Sumter, Lincoln called out seventy-five thousand militia, carefully cloaking the call in constitutional wrapping: "Now, therefore, I, Abraham Lincoln, President of the United States, in virtue of the power in me vested by the Constitution, and the laws. . . ." He used the same wording to invoke his constitutional power to convene a special session of Congress on July 4. That was the most nationalistic day of the year, and Lincoln was trying to manage the nation's response to the war by tying it to the Constitution, which he had already said contained no authority for secession. On April 19, ratcheting up the pressure on the Southerners, Lincoln proclaimed a naval blockade of the Confederate states "until Congress shall have assembled and deliberated." Lincoln was not afraid to act independently of Congress, but he made it clear that he wanted the legislature involved, as the Constitution required.[12]

Lincoln's federalization of the militia saw enthusiastic responses from the Northern states, but in protest, four more Southern states joined the secession movement. Virginia led the way, followed in later weeks by Arkansas, North Carolina, and Tennessee. Kentucky, Maryland, Missouri, and Delaware, all slave states, remained on the fence. Would they also secede and join the Confederacy? They never did.

The threat of Maryland's departure from the Union grew particularly grave when the first militia unit Lincoln had mobilized tried to reach Washington. The most direct route from the Northern states into Washington was through Maryland, particularly through Baltimore. On April 19, troops of the 6th Massachusetts Regiment steamed into Baltimore by train from the North. The railroad ran into President Street Station, and horses then pulled the cars full of soldiers to Camden Station, from which the train would travel into Washington. Crowds began to gather and attack the horse-drawn cars. The soldiers were ordered out and marched along the streets. A riot ensued, shots were fired, and people died—four Union soldiers and twelve Confederate supporters.

It looked as though the militia would never make it to Washington. "Why don't they come! Why don't they come!" Lincoln cried out to no one in particular one day. Fortunately for him, the militia finally arrived. Several delegations of Marylanders also came to Washington to try to persuade him not to send any more troops through Baltimore in order to avoid further violence. At first Lincoln agreed to that proposal, even though those around him thought it made no sense. Thinking better of it, Lincoln then told one of his secretaries "that this was the last time he was going to interfere in matters of strictly military concernment. That he would leave them hereafter wholly to military men."[13]

The more he thought about the attack on Federal troops peacefully marching through Baltimore, the angrier Lincoln became. Speaking to a delegation of Baltimore YMCA leaders who came to visit him, he reacted to their call for keeping militia out of the city by almost shouting: "You would have me break my oath and surrender the Government without a blow. There is no Washington in that—no Jackson in that—no manhood nor honor in that. . . . Our men are not moles, and can't dig under the earth; they are not birds, and can't fly through the air. There is no way but to march across, and that they must do. . . . Keep your rowdies in Baltimore, and there will be no bloodshed." Repeating his Fort Sumter position, he said, "If they will not attack us, we will not attack them; but if they do attack us, we will return it, and that severely."[14]

The second military unit, the 8th Massachusetts Regiment, soon made it safely through Annapolis without incident, but Lincoln still worried. He told Scott again to be ready to suspend the writ of habeas corpus along the railroad line between Philadelphia and Baltimore. He also widened the naval blockade; called for 43,034 more volunteers, this time for three years, not just ninety days as the Militia Act of 1795 required; and increased the size of the regular army. Lincoln promised to submit all such executive orders to Congress when it came into session. He called on all citizens to accept his pronouncement "for the effectual suppression of unlawful violence, for the impartial enforcement of constitutional laws, and for the speediest possible restoration of peace and order."[15]

While being so concerned about the safety of Washington, DC, and Maryland remaining in the Union, Lincoln also took action in the region across the Appalachian Mountains, determined to try to ensure that his home state, Kentucky, remained in the Union. He ordered Robert Anderson, the hero of Fort Sumter, to go to Kentucky and enlist as many three-year volunteers there as he could. He told his secretary of war that he wanted the four Missouri German regiments that had already been raised made into a brigade and placed under the command of Carl Schurz, one the nation's major German immigrant political leaders.[16] The Germans were loyal to the Union and could offer many fighting men. Lincoln wanted their support cemented to the cause as soon as possible.

Lincoln thus began to grapple with a problem he was to face throughout the war: political generals. These were politicians who had little or no military experience but were leaders in their communities with the influence necessary to persuade others to enlist. They might not have the ability to excel on the battlefields, but without these men, it is difficult to imagine the Union army reaching the numbers it did. Even Grant and Sherman, although they were West Pointers, received their initial appointments because they had political connections.[17]

Lincoln now demonstrated his impatience with the slow-moving nature of the Federal war effort, an attitude he would express many times in the years ahead. In his usual quiet, nonthreatening way, he wondered whether the Federals should take Alexandria and Arlington Heights, Virginia, immediately. Winfield Scott listened, and Union troops soon occupied those places—which included Robert E. Lee's domicile. Because an officer was killed in this May 1861 movement, Lincoln wrote a letter of condolence to the man's family, not unlike many such letters he had to write throughout the war. This early one was particularly poignant because the dead man, Elmer E. Ellsworth, was Lincoln's friend.[18]

General Benjamin F. Butler, a leading Massachusetts politician who commanded at Fort Monroe, at the base of the James River peninsula, now wanted to dislodge Confederate outposts at nearby Little and Big Bethel. The thirty-five hundred ill-organized Union troops attacked the entrenched twelve hundred Confederate troops on June 10, 1861, and were repulsed all along the line and on the flank, suffering a disproportionate seventy-nine-to-eight casualty rate.[19]

Having had the war brought home to him in the death of his friend and the repulse at Big Bethel, Lincoln tried even harder to build up the still tiny Federal army. He promoted eight officers but was unhappy that "nearly one fourth of the whole" came from just one state, New York. This was no way to ensure national loyalty, Lincoln understood. He also supported Jim Lane as a leader of Kansas troops, even though Lane was a loose cannon at best. Once again, Lincoln authorized Scott or anyone designated by him to suspend the writ of habeas corpus when necessary.[20]

Up to this point, Lincoln had acted alone, but now he had to face a special session of Congress regarding all the proclamations he had made with only the promise that the legislature would evaluate them once it came back into session in July. Congress was now one-third smaller than it had been when Southern state representatives were still present, and it was now two-thirds Republican. On July 5, the congressmen and senators considered Lincoln's message to them. The president lambasted secession, calling it an unconstitutional "sophism," and pointed out that even before he had taken office, the so-called Confederate States had been established to oppose the United States. In his inaugural address, he had promised not to take any military action unless forced to do so. The Confederate attack on

Fort Sumter had demonstrated that the Southern states were more interested in separation than in peace. He had taken the actions he had in order to prevent the crumbling of the Union. He now asked Congress to grant him four hundred thousand more men and $400 million to put down the insurrection, but then he did little to try to influence its decision.

Congress gave Lincoln five hundred thousand soldiers and $500 million to prosecute the war, and in twenty-nine working days, it passed seventy-six bills, all but four dealing with the war. Congress ratified Lincoln's earlier call for seventy-five thousand militia men, as well as his naval blockade, expansion of the regular army, suspension of habeas corpus in selected areas, and use of public moneys for military purposes. The legislative branch accepted Lincoln's expansion of powers at their expense, although they did so most reluctantly. It was not until the last day of the session, August 6, 1861, that Congress actually validated all of Lincoln's previous proclamations. The legislation did so as unobtrusively as possible, as part of an "act to increase the Pay of the Privates." Congress demonstrated unity on the direction of the war, although many senators and representatives believed Lincoln's acts violated the Constitution. Lincoln came out of the special session of Congress stronger than he had gone in. He could readily see that the usual conflict between congressional and presidential control of a war had been decided in his favor, this early in the conflict.[21]

While Congress deliberated, the impatience of the nation to put the South in its place influenced these deliberations. The war had not gone the way most Northerners, including the president and Congress, had assumed it would. Lincoln remained upset at the lethargy of his army, and the press was even more demanding. Led by Horace Greeley's powerful *New York Tribune,* the press had become insistent from the time of Lincoln's first call for volunteers that the army act decisively and end this war quickly. From Lincoln on down, Northerners naively believed that secession had been the work of a vociferous minority, so they thought an overwhelming dose of shot and shell would fire up the Southern Unionists and quickly bring the states back into the Union.

It was on May 30, while Horace Greeley was away at his farm recuperating from an ax wound to his knee, that his newspaper stated the words that would always be associated with him: "On to Richmond." Within a month, the paper's masthead repeated every day, "Forward to Richmond! Forward to Richmond!" The *Tribune*, now under the leadership of Charles A. Dana, a later assistant secretary of war, also demanded the resignation of Lincoln's entire cabinet. Rival papers, favorable to Lincoln, were incensed. The loyal states were now splitting over the war's direction.[22]

The *Tribune*'s demand that the Federals take Richmond before the Confederate Congress could meet there received a favorable public hearing because of the overwhelming belief in the Federal army's superiority. Winfield Scott and most army officers insisted that the army needed more preparation before going into action, but Lincoln believed that although his army might not be totally prepared, neither was the other side. He decided that the Federal army had to go on the offensive.

General Irvin McDowell was put in command of the field army, which, during the special session of Congress in mid-July, began its movement toward Manassas Junction, an important railroad crossing, fronted by Bull Run. McDowell organized his thirty-thousand-man force into five divisions. The Confederates under General P. G. T. Beauregard were smaller and less organized. They consisted of the Confederate Army of the Potomac under Beauregard and the separate distant Army of the Shenandoah under General Joseph E. Johnston. These two armies totaled around thirty thousand men, but Johnston's troops were in the Shenandoah Valley, with Union general Robert Patterson's force at least capable of blocking their movement toward Bull Run.

Displaying the similarity of Union and Confederate military thinking, both McDowell and Beauregard tried to implement the same battle plan: a feint on the other army's right flank and an attack in force on the enemy's left flank. Had both armies attacked at the same time, the result would have been a reversal of their initial positions. As it was, McDowell was much more successful than Beauregard in getting his flanking movement started, and Federal troops began to drive the Confederates. The chaotic march from Washington and the long attack movement, however, soon took the energy out of McDowell's men. Then Patterson's failure to keep Johnston bottled up in the Shenandoah Valley resulted in an infusion of Confederate reinforcements at a crucial time in the battle. An eccentric professor from the Virginia Military Institute, Thomas Jackson, had his unit determinedly stand "like a stonewall" and further stymied the Federal attack. This earned him the nickname Stonewall Jackson.

The tide of battle reversed, and exhausted Federal soldiers began drifting toward the rear until their retreat turned into a rout. Washingtonians who had come out in carriages to see the great Union victory watched their army falling to the rear and became entangled with the running soldiers. Fortunately for the Federals, the Confederates were as disorganized and exhausted as they were, so an effective pursuit proved impossible. Confederate generals and President Jefferson Davis unfairly took a great deal of criticism for not pursuing the Federals and taking Washington. In fact, the Confederates had won a victory and provided an enormous shock to the Federals.[23]

Lincoln was terribly disappointed with the results of this first major battle. As he was to do throughout the war, though, whether in times of triumph or defeat, he looked to see what he could learn from the experience. He sat down and outlined his next steps to organize the Union effort for future victory: his government had to increase the effectiveness of the blockade; continue preparing the forces under political general Benjamin Butler at Fort Monroe; hold on to Baltimore; strengthen the army in the Shenandoah Valley, western Virginia, and Missouri; and discharge the three-month soldiers as quickly as possible and organize those with longer stints. Lincoln wrote this memo to himself just two days after the battle, and it clearly demonstrated his major concern: the protection of Washington.[24]

Four days later, he had two more thoughts, and one of these demonstrated that he had come to realize that the war was not simply going to be fought and decided in the area between Washington and Richmond. He wanted that region's railroads controlled by the capture of Manassas or some other key spot, but then he added, "This done, a joint movement from Cairo on Memphis: and from Cincinnati on East Tennessee."[25] Lincoln still did not see how vast this war was going to become and that capturing places would not result in victory. His inexperience and his dependence on military leaders remained the greatest influences on him, but he had already demonstrated that he, not Congress or the military, was going to lead the Northern military effort. The reluctant antiwar Whig had already moved beyond the thinking of his earlier years, but he had a long way to go before he could provide the military leadership the nation needed.

CHAPTER THREE

"THE INTEGRITY OF THE UNION [IS] PROMINENT"

Likely remembering his Black Hawk War experience, Lincoln demonstrated that he was going to be a hands-on military leader. Several days after the disaster at Bull Run, on July 21, 1861, he visited Union troops to offer encouragement. He stopped by the New York 69th Volunteer Regiment, part of the brigade of Colonel William Tecumseh Sherman, an inexperienced officer unhappy with his green troops' recent performance. A subordinate officer had told Sherman that he had already served his time and was leaving for home. The colonel threatened to shoot him if he tried. Sherman was nearly as firm with the president during Lincoln's visit. To Lincoln's amusement, the colonel told him not to encourage the soldiers to get overly excited at his presence. When Lincoln later toured the brigade in his carriage, he repeated, "Don't cheer, boys, I confess I rather like it myself, but Colonel Sherman says it is not military; and I guess we better defer to his opinion."

The disgruntled officer immediately told Lincoln about Sherman's threat. Lincoln bent over close to the man and, in a voice that could be heard all over the unit, said, "Well, if I were you, and he threatened to shoot [me], I would not trust him, for I believe he would do it." Sherman nodded in approval, and the soldiers laughed uproariously. More importantly, they demonstrated their support for their president by reenlisting in large numbers.[1] Lincoln's personal touch was effective.

Lincoln also became directly involved in a host of other details as he tried to get the Union military effort on track. He told Winfield Scott to evaluate an individual who was encouraging the army to use his hot air balloons for observation of the enemy. He tried to soothe the feelings of Maryland congressmen about the army's need to search their constituents to ensure security against Confederate sympathizers. He tried to get Secretary of War Simon Cameron to quickly promote a list of individuals to higher rank, and the following day, he specifically wanted Cameron to promote Ulysses S. Grant to brigadier general. Later he included William T. Sherman's nomination too, no doubt at the urging of Thomas Ewing, an important Whig politician and Sherman's father-in-law. Lincoln allowed Massachusetts political general Benjamin Butler to raise a brigade of five thousand men, increasing that number to six thousand in early September. He appointed old friend and Illinois politician John A. McClernand to be a brigadier general and lead a new brigade of Illinois volunteers. To make sure that military men would not provide intelligence to the enemy, Lincoln reminded them of the 57th Article of War, prohibiting such activity on threat of execution. And to invoke God's blessing on the Union cause, he proclaimed a day of fast for the last Thursday of September. Lincoln tried to make sure he covered every possibility to improve the Federal war effort.[2]

Then he was unexpectedly faced with a major crisis. In the West, General John C. Fremont, the 1856 Republican candidate for the presidency, was doing a poor job. To add to his miscues, Fremont issued a proclamation on August 30 indicating that he would execute prisoners of war and liberate the slaves of individuals opposed to the Federal government. Lincoln told him that the freeing of any slaves would "alarm our Southern Union friends, and turn them against us." Besides, as president, he would make such decisions himself.[3]

"The Pathfinder's" intelligent and beautiful wife, Jessie Benton Fremont, who was the daughter of the influential senator Thomas Hart Benton, rushed to Washington to protest Lincoln's annulment of her husband's orders. Lincoln listened impatiently to her and then refused to accept her argument. Lincoln believed that Fremont's freeing of the slaves was "*purely political*, and not within the range of *military* law, or necessity." A general or a president who "may make permanent rules of property by proclamation" was subverting a "government of Constitution and laws." Ironically, Lincoln made this statement exactly one year before he issued the Emancipation Proclamation. At that later time, he argued that he had the right to emancipate slaves, based on his constitutional war powers.[4]

As he grappled with the Fremont problem, Lincoln continued to worry about Kentucky. He knew its possession was crucial to the Union cause and to the safety of Unionists in East Tennessee, a concern that stayed with him for most of the war. He asked the hero of Fort Sumter, Robert Anderson, whom he had sent to Kentucky in May to raise troops, to organize the war effort there formally. Anderson called a friend to go with him to see the president. Lincoln asked William T. Sherman to serve in Kentucky too, and Sherman made it clear that he would serve only as Anderson's subordinate. He got Lincoln to promise never to put him into a command position. Lincoln laughingly said that there were not enough command slots anyway, so Sherman could have his wish.[5]

Lincoln wanted Kentucky to be kept in the Union because he believed that the war could be won there. He wrote a detailed memorandum on October 1, 1861, explaining how he wanted the conflict waged there. Union troops were to go on the move around October 5. One force would take and secure the Cumberland Gap, while the other, a joint army-navy force, headed for Port Royal, South Carolina. Once these movements were under way, George B. McClellan in western Virginia and John C. Fremont in Missouri should "avail themselves of any advantages the diversions may present" and move forward.[6] Early in the war, therefore, Lincoln was urging attacks on multiple fronts, ignoring the mass movements advocated by contemporary military theory and, even more important, by his generals. Lincoln was gaining his footing.

Fremont did not move, however, and Lincoln lost patience and fired him on November 2. Lincoln's instructions to his replacement, General Samuel R. Curtis, showed what the president had wanted from Fremont. Lincoln offered "a few *suggestions*" recognizing, he said, that it is "hazardous . . . to bind down a distant commander in the field to specific lines and operations." But he did so anyway. He told Curtis to give up trying to catch Confederate general Sterling Price. Instead, Curtis should divide his army in two and learn what he could from their observations. He should also guard the railroads, recruit more soldiers, and perfect what equipment they had as they waited for new matériel to arrive. If Curtis did that, he would have a "surplus of force," which he could then move around as needed. If, on the other hand, he continued chasing Price, "by this long and circuitous route, to reach Memphis," this effort would be "exhaustive beyond endurance, and . . . end in the loss of the whole force engaged in it."[7]

Confusion was thus rampant in both the West and the East. Unhappy with the lack of energy displayed by Winfield Scott, Lincoln turned to George B. McClellan, the victor over Robert E. Lee in western Virginia. Lincoln's idea was for Scott to remain as overall general in chief, while McClellan became the commander of a field army, the Army of the Potomac. But McClellan accused the old general of thwarting his plans for victory and effectively forced Scott out. McClellan then became overall commander at one month shy of age thirty-five.

When McClellan took over after Scott retired and left Washington, Lincoln worried that the task might be too great even for someone as talented as McClellan. "I should be perfectly satisfied," Lincoln said to his young commander on November 1, "if I thought that this vast increase of responsibility would not embarrass you." McClellan said it would not. "I can do it all," he told Lincoln.[8]

And he certainly meant that. He proved unwilling to take advice from anyone, including the president, whom he considered "nothing more than a well meaning baboon." McClellan's disrespect of the president was obvious. In mid-November, Lincoln, Secretary of State William H. Seward, and the president's secretary John Hay went to McClellan's house. He was away at a wedding, and the three men waited an hour for him to return. When he did, he ignored them and went upstairs to his room. Another period of time passed by, until the president's entourage sent word that they were still waiting. A servant came down the stairs and said that the general had gone to bed. Hay was furious, but Lincoln characteristically responded that "it was better at this time not to be making points of etiquette & personal dignity." Lincoln believed that he needed McClellan, so he was willing to ignore his boorish behavior.[9]

As the days and weeks dragged on without any movement from the Army of the Potomac, however, Lincoln grew increasingly impatient with McClellan. The young general continued to train his force, while bemoaning that it was much too small. Lincoln sent him a memo asking some pointed questions. If a decision were made to put the Army of the Potomac on the offensive, for example, "how *long* would it require to actually get in motion?" Lincoln then presented detailed advice to McClellan on how he might go on the offensive immediately. McClellan brushed off Lincoln's strategic thoughts and responded, "I have now my mind actively turned towards another plan of campaign that I do not think at all anticipated by the enemy nor by many of our own people."[10] In short, McClellan was still making preparations. He had no plans to attack immediately.

While Lincoln worried about the war in general and McClellan in particular, he also had to govern the nation as a whole. His annual message to Congress on December 3, 1861, demonstrated that almost everything he did was somehow connected to the war effort. He happily reported that, as of July 1 of that year, there was a surplus in the Treasury of more than $2 million. "It is gratifying to know that the expenditures made necessary by the rebellion are not beyond the resources of the loyal people," he wrote. He also gave Congress his philosophy of war: "In considering the policy to be adopted for suppressing the insurrection, I have been anxious and careful that the inevitable conflict for this purpose shall not degenerate into a violent and remorseless revolutionary struggle. I have, therefore, in every case, thought it proper to keep the integrity of the Union prominent as the primary object of the contest on our part, leaving all questions [slavery] which are not of vital military importance to the more deliberate action of the legislature."[11]

As the first year of the war came to a close, then, Lincoln's annual address was positive, but the reality was more negative. The new commanding general, George B. McClellan, showed no disposition to move. Then he became ill with typhoid fever and had to take to his bed, making any hope of progress in the Virginia theater even more remote. In the West, Generals Henry W. Halleck and Don Carlos Buell had responsibility for the vast area in the middle of the nation, but when Lincoln asked them to cooperate in a forward movement, both responded that McClellan had not provided them with any such orders. Besides, they did not believe that the time was ripe for cooperation, because there was too much preparation to accomplish first. The war remained a stalemate in both the East and the West, and this fact continued to benefit the Confederacy.[12]

Lincoln refused to take no for an answer. He continued to demand movement. He told Halleck that he wanted him to cooperate with Buell "at once." Getting only a negative reaction, Lincoln pointedly requested, "Please name as early a day as you safely can, or before which you can be ready to move Southward in concert with Gen. Buell. Delay is ruining us." He frustratedly cried out to Quartermaster General Montgomery Meigs on January 10, 1862, "The people are impatient, [Secretary of the Treasury Salmon P.] Chase has no money . . . the General of the Army [George B. McClellan] has typhoid fever. The bottom is out of the tub. What shall I do?"[13]

Generals were not the only problem; politicians were also hurting the war effort. Secretary of War Simon Cameron was proving inept in his duties, and Lincoln decided he had to remove him. Ever careful not to make political enemies, however, the president reminded Cameron of his earlier desire to resign his post and told him that if he did, Lincoln would send him as minister to St. Petersburg, Russia. Cameron accepted this diplomatic post, and on January 15, 1862, Lincoln made one of the most significant military decisions of the war: he named Edwin M. Stanton to be his new secretary of war. Stanton was one of the nation's leading lawyers and a man who, at an earlier time, had expressed dim respect for fellow attorney Abraham Lincoln. When James Buchanan's administration was on the verge of unraveling, Stanton became its attorney general in December 1860 and helped it finish with a modicum of stability. In the early months of Lincoln's presidency, the Democrat Stanton had frequently lambasted the Republican Lincoln for a lack of policy. Yet for the good of the nation, Lincoln ignored Stanton's sharp criticism and put him in his cabinet. From this point on, next to Lincoln, Stanton was the most militarily influential political leader in the nation.[14]

It did not take long for the new team of Lincoln and Stanton to act. Lincoln bluntly told Halleck and Buell that massing troops on a particular point was not the way to fight the war. The Union army should use its "superior forces at *different* points, at the *same* time." Getting nowhere with cajoling his generals, Lincoln issued President's General War Order No. 1 on January 27. He told the entire military, army and navy, that it had to move no later than February 22, 1862, Washington's birthday. The military leadership was unhappy with this ultimatum, but because it came from the commander in chief, they had to obey, or at least appear to be doing so.[15]

There was a young officer in the West who agreed with Lincoln about the lethargy of the western command. Ulysses S. Grant wanted to move against Confederate general Albert Sidney Johnston's defense line, strung out from the Cumberland Gap in the East to Columbus, Kentucky, in the West. He continued pestering Halleck for a meeting so that he might present his plan. Halleck kept refusing, but when Grant finally met with him, Halleck sent him off with a wave of his hand. Grant did not give up, however, demonstrating the determination that would prove to be so important later in the war. He called on U.S. Navy flag officer Andrew Foote to join him in pressuring Halleck, and thanks, no doubt, to Lincoln's determination to get Union forces in motion by February 22, Halleck allowed Grant and Foote to attack the Tennessee River's Fort Henry.

This fort fell on February 6, 1862, and Grant followed up that victory by taking the Cumberland River's Fort Donelson on February 16. When Grant refused any terms but "unconditional surrender" for the capitulation of the Confederates at Donelson, he acquired a new nickname—"Unconditional Surrender Grant"—and the nation gained a new hero. Lincoln noticed. When he signed Grant's nomination to major general, he said, "If the Southerners think that man for man they are better than our Illinois men, or Western men generally, they will discover themselves in a grievous mistake."[16]

Despite Grant's success and Lincoln's feeling of satisfaction with him, Henry W. Halleck was not impressed. Grant might have won important victories, but his commanding officer did not consider him a competent general. Halleck believed that Grant did not file his reports as required and, in a pique, fired him. Lincoln demanded to know what was going on, and rather than debate the president, Halleck brought Grant back. Lincoln did not know it at the time, but he had saved Grant's military career and allowed him to continue to grow as a leader.[17]

These two Grant victories broke Johnston's defense line, and he had to pull back to Corinth, Mississippi, where a north-south and an east-west railroad crossed. Brigadier General Samuel R. Curtis, commander of the Army of Southwest Missouri, ensured that state for the Union with a victory at Pea Ridge, Arkansas, in early March 1862. By mid-March, General John Pope had captured New Madrid on the Mississippi River, and Don Carlos Buell had walked into Nashville unopposed. Halleck had not led one soldier into battle, but the generals under him, like U. S. Grant, were winning victory after victory. In the East, meanwhile, McClellan was still debating Lincoln about his need for more troops. Halleck was the only Federal commander pressing forward against the enemy.

With Stanton's help, Lincoln continued arguing with McClellan about the necessity of movement in the East. McClellan kept insisting that he needed more soldiers and more of everything else before he could move on Richmond, the capital of the Confederacy. When he felt ready, he said, he wanted to move by ship to the base of the James River peninsula and then push up that land mass to Richmond. Conversely, Lincoln believed that McClellan already had enough soldiers and should attack immediately and straight forward toward Richmond.

To concentrate McClellan's focus on the task ahead, Lincoln stripped him of the office of commanding general on March 11. He kept McClellan as leader of the Army of the Potomac, while he and Stanton took on the responsibility for directing the entire war. Abraham Lincoln had begun the war believing that his military knowledge was inferior to that of the professionals commanding his armies, but he had experienced an obvious change of mind. The foot dragging of so many of his generals and their insistence that they had to prepare, prepare, prepare before they could go on the offensive convinced him that he had to step in and directly push them forward.

The issue of protecting Washington from Confederate attack was a particular matter of debate between McClellan and Lincoln, and it was never definitively decided. Even before McClellan's army finally began its March 17, 1862, move on the Virginia Peninsula, Lincoln was not satisfied that McClellan had obeyed his order to leave a sufficient force to protect Washington, DC. On April 3, exasperated and fearful, Lincoln ordered Secretary of War Stanton to protect Washington by holding back one corps from McClellan's attacking force.[18]

Lincoln now took another major step. He carefully expressed his belief that this war was about slavery as much as it was about the Union. His respect for the Constitution prevented him from saying so forthrightly, so he began chipping away at the institution, always framing each one of his gradual and subtle attacks as part of the war to preserve the Union. The previous spring, on May 23, 1861, General Benjamin Butler had anticipated antislavery action when he had told a Confederate army officer that the officer's demand for the return of his fugitive slaves under the provisions of the Fugitive Slave Law was not valid. These slaves had been worked as part of the Confederate war effort, so they were "contraband of war" and could be properly seized under the laws of war. Now Lincoln sent Congress a suggestion for a joint resolution: "Resolved that the United States ought to co-operate with any state which may adopt a gradual abolishment of slavery," providing such states with "pecuniary aid." Spurred by this statement, Congress eradicated slavery in the District of Columbia, with Lincoln signing the law on April 16, 1862.[19]

Lincoln also had to deal with a personal tragedy around this time that had an impact on his war leadership. Early in 1862, eleven-year-old Willie Lincoln became ill, and he died in the White House on February 20. His father and mother were devastated, with Mary perhaps never recovering from the loss, and the president having to fight through his anguish. Lincoln did not lose a son in combat, as so many Americans of that age did, but with Willie's death, he experienced the sorrow of the sudden loss of a loved one and thus could identify with the tragedy of war-related death as never before.

Meanwhile, in the West, Ulysses S. Grant's Army of the Tennessee was camped at Pittsburg Landing, Tennessee, awaiting the arrival of Don Carlos Buell's Army of the Ohio. As soon as these units arrived, Halleck would merge them and lead them against the important railroad city of Corinth, Mississippi, twenty-two miles away. Albert Sidney Johnston's army was behind entrenchments there, and the battle would be hard, but no Union soldier doubted a Union victory. Halleck's plan was completely old-school: to mass his troops and capture an important railroad center.

It did not happen that way. Johnston surprised Grant (and one of his division commanders, William T. Sherman) by leaving his entrenchments, marching the twenty-two miles north, and launching an attack on the Federals at Shiloh. The first day, the Confederates nearly drove Grant's army into the Tennessee River, but Albert Sidney Johnston died in the process. On the second day, Grant rallied his troops and merged them with those of Don Carlos Buell, who had arrived the evening before, and the combined Union army drove the Confederates back toward Corinth.

The casualties were horrific on both sides, and a sensationalist press fed lurid tales to the nation. Once more, accusations against Grant, the drunk, and Crazy Sherman surfaced. Pressure fell on Lincoln to remove Grant immediately. Exasperated, he had Stanton telegraph Halleck, who by this time had arrived at Shiloh and was preparing the massed army to march on Corinth. Lincoln wanted to know "whether any neglect or misconduct of General Grant or any other officer contributed to the sad casualties that befell our forces on Sunday."[20]

Halleck refused to provide any answers because, he said, he had not yet received all the proper paperwork from his subordinates.[21] Shiloh was a victory, after all, and at about the same time, John Pope had taken Island Number Ten in the Mississippi River, and Admiral David Farragut was in the process of completing the capture of New Orleans.

It only got better. John Pope's army joined Grant's and Buell's forces at Shiloh, and under Halleck's methodical leadership, the troops moved on Corinth. The Union army took the city at the end of May 1862, although Halleck allowed Beauregard's Confederates to escape, relying on traditional military theory that places, not armies, mattered. As a result, though, Memphis was outflanked, and in early June, it succumbed to a Union flotilla. Halleck continued the Union's winning ways in the West.

Unfortunately for Lincoln, his generals were not doing as well in the East, but the Confederates were. McClellan continued to dither, and Stonewall Jackson was conducting a successful Shenandoah Valley campaign. Then on May 9, a general took an action that Lincoln found harmful to the Union cause. General David Hunter, now commanding the Department of the South, which consisted of Georgia, Florida, and South Carolina, "declared forever free" slaves in his department. As he had earlier responded to John C. Fremont's pronouncement, Lincoln quickly pronounced Hunter's statement "void" on May 19. He repeated again that it was his responsibility, and his alone, to deal with this issue, and if in the future "it shall have become a necessity indispensable to the maintenance of the government" to free the slaves, he would make that decision himself. Besides, earlier that year, on March 6, Congress had passed the joint resolution he had earlier suggested, giving "pecuniary aid" to any free state wishing to gradually abolish slavery. He called on the slave states to take advantage of this opportunity quickly. "The change it contemplates would come gently as the dews of heaven, not rending or wrecking anything. Will you not embrace it? . . . You cannot if you would, be blind to the signs of the times." Once again, Lincoln tied slavery into the war, and he continued to keep presidential control over the issue.[22]

As always, however, McClellan remained Lincoln's major problem. He did not begin his movement up the Peninsula until April 4, just two days before the battle at Shiloh. Early on, it became obvious that McClellan was still overly concerned about his opposition, led by General Joseph E. Johnston. Lincoln tried to encourage him. "I have never written you, or spoken to you, in greater kindness of feeling than now, nor with a fuller purpose to sustain you," he said. "*But*," Lincoln insisted, "*you must act*." When McClellan ran into a force under "Prince John" Magruder at Yorktown, Virginia, he became convinced that he was outnumbered, even though he had fifty thousand troops to the Confederates' ten thousand. Instead of attacking, he began a siege that lasted for almost a month, until the theatrical Magruder and his men slipped away. Although the Confederates were holding the Federals back at Williamsburg long enough for the city of Richmond to be supplied, McClellan's forces still found themselves so near Richmond that the soldiers could hear church bells. Nevertheless, McClellan continued to be cautious, kept finding fault with Washington's support, and blamed everyone but himself for anything that did not meet his expectations. He did not move on the city.[23]

Lincoln did experience some personal military success, however. During the Federal drive to capture Norfolk, he was visiting that area and chose what he felt was the best place to land troops. The result was the capture of the city and the Confederate necessity to destroy the ironclad *Merrimack* to keep it out of Union hands.[24] It was almost as though Lincoln were trying to show his generals how to fight this war, but as yet, no one seemed to be watching.

Thankfully for McClellan, Confederate general Joseph E. Johnston mishandled his force during the two-day Battle of Seven Pines (Fair Oaks) on May 31–June 1, 1862, and McClellan's army handed the Confederates a bloody defeat. Even Johnston was injured and incapacitated. Amazingly, though, McClellan did not continue his attack but called for more troops and waited for the weather to become just right for an offensive.

Robert E. Lee now took the injured Johnston's place, and in the Seven Days Campaign from June 25 to July 1, while the Federals inflicted severe casualties on the Confederates, more than 20,000 compared with 15,800, Lee pushed McClellan away from Richmond and saved the city. The question was, what should the Federal army do next? Lincoln reached back to a former adviser to try to find out. Winfield Scott was living at West Point, and on June 23, even before the beginning of the Seven Days Campaign, Lincoln traveled to see Scott and ask his advice. Perhaps the old veteran could provide a clue to the Federal puzzle. Scott's advice to Lincoln is unknown, but on June 26, Lincoln issued an order establishing a new Army of Virginia under John Pope, combining the forces presently commanded by Generals John C. Fremont, Nathaniel Banks, Irvin McDowell, and Samuel Sturgis. The new army's job was to protect western Virginia and Washington "from danger or insult," defeat the Confederate armies led by Generals Stonewall Jackson and Richard Ewell, harass the Confederates near Chancellorsville, "and render the most effective aid to relieve General McClellan and capture Richmond." In short, Pope's and McClellan's armies were clearly to cooperate against the Confederates in the Old Dominion.[25]

At that same time, Lincoln told his secretary of state that the Union army should hold its gains in the West, take control of the Mississippi River, occupy East Tennessee to aid the Unionists there, capture Chattanooga, and keep a force near Washington to protect the capital. To do all this, Lincoln decided that he needed 100,000 more soldiers, adding for emphasis, "I expect to maintain this contest until successful, or till I die, or am conquered, or my term expires, or Congress or the country forsakes me." Lincoln actually asked the nation for 150,000 more soldiers, and on July 1, he raised that number to 300,000.[26]

When McClellan heard of Lincoln's action, he called on the president to send him fifty thousand more soldiers. Lincoln exploded. "The idea of sending you fifty thousand, or any other considerable force promptly, is simply absurd," he said. He then wrote to Halleck, "Please tell me, could you make a flying visit for consultation without endangering the service in your Department?"[27]

Lincoln was plainly unhappy with the sloth of George B. McClellan and pleased at the recurring successes in the West. Like most Americans, he gave most of the credit to Henry W. Halleck. That was why he asked Halleck to come to Washington. At the same time, Lincoln visited McClellan and interviewed all his subordinates. It could not have been clearer. Lincoln wanted help in running the war. He and Stanton had been working under a heavy burden and making little progress, at least in the East. On July 11, 1862, the president appointed a new general in chief: Henry W. Halleck.[28] Lincoln hoped to put all his military burdens on the shoulders of a successful military man who he thought could solve them.

C H A P T E R   F O U R

"WITHOUT SLAVERY THE REBELLION COULD NEVER HAVE EXISTED"

Abraham Lincoln had thought that acting as general in chief, with Secretary of War Stanton's aid, would allow George McClellan to concentrate on commanding the Army of the Potomac. McClellan had not changed any of his behavior, however, and he continued to insist that he did not have enough troops to do his job and thus could not move forward against Richmond. The result was that he was stymied on the Peninsula.

So Lincoln turned to Henry W. Halleck to take over the task of being commanding general, to use the skill in the East that he had demonstrated in the West.[1] Lincoln was more than happy to let Halleck make the technical military decisions. He knew what should happen; all he needed was a general to do it. Despite his ambition, Halleck was not so sure he wanted the post, and he also worried about alienating McClellan, a man he admired. He was slow in coming to Washington, as if to delay taking the reins of military power. This was hardly an encouraging sign.

Lincoln wanted Halleck to break the stalemate on the Peninsula immediately. "I am very anxious to have you here," he wrote, but Halleck continued delaying, trying to make sure he left everything in the West just right. He did not leave Mississippi for Washington until July 20, 1862, and he did not arrive in the nation's capital until July 23. He wrote fulsome letters of good-bye to his subordinates, and Grant and Sherman, among them, wrote letters full of praise in response. Grant mentioned Halleck's "gigantic intellect" and admitted that although he and Halleck had had "several little spats," he "like[d] and respect[ed] him nevertheless." Others viewed Halleck differently, however. Secretary of the Navy Gideon Welles wrote in his diary, Halleck's "mind is heavy and irresolute," and Admiral Andrew Foote was even more critical, telling Welles that Halleck was "a military imbecile."[2]

As soon as he arrived at the capital, Halleck met with Lincoln; Secretary of War Edwin M. Stanton; General John Pope, commander of the newly organized Army of Virginia; and Ambrose Burnside, commander of the new IX Corps of the Army of the Potomac. Lincoln made it clear that he was unhappy with McClellan. With Halleck, his new commanding general, listening, Lincoln offered command of the Army of the Potomac to Burnside. But that general said no and praised McClellan, so Lincoln backed off. Lincoln then gave Halleck full authority to fire McClellan or keep him on. He warned his new commanding general, however, that McClellan would demand more soldiers before he agreed to do anything. Halleck had to be ready for that.

When they met in Virginia on July 25, Halleck was impressed with the charismatic McClellan. He hesitatingly said he was there "to ascertain from him his views and wishes in regard to future operations." McClellan proposed taking his army behind Richmond to cut off the Confederate supply line instead of going after the city itself. Halleck spoke up, echoing the principles he had emphasized in his important book on military strategy and tactics. He said it was "a military necessity" for McClellan to mass with John Pope's new Army of Virginia and capture one militarily significant place, Richmond, while shielding another, Washington, from capture.

Thinking that he and McClellan were in agreement, Halleck went back to Washington and immediately reported to Lincoln. At almost the same time, Halleck received a telegram from McClellan indicating that before he could attack, he needed every fighting man in the East and twenty thousand men from the West besides. Halleck was aghast, but Lincoln likely was thinking, I told you so.

Halleck's response to McClellan's demand proved weak and lost him any hope he had of commanding "Little Mac." He did not tell

McClellan what his subordinate needed to do; instead, he begged McClellan to cooperate with him. Both men reflected the contemporary military thinking of that age. Halleck wanted to mass two armies and then go on the attack against a smaller enemy force, while McClellan did not believe he had enough soldiers to create a mass large enough to overwhelm the enemy, whose numbers he exaggerated. He thought his only hope was to destroy Confederate communications and supply through a flanking movement to the Confederate rear. Both men wanted to take Richmond, and both believed that the capital city, and not the army in front of it, was their target.

After repeated disagreement in letters and telegrams, Halleck put his foot down. He ordered McClellan to leave the Peninsula, mass with Pope, and attack Richmond. McClellan pleaded with Halleck to rescind the order. Halleck said no and tried to persuade McClellan, using arguments found in his textbook. Lincoln had to have liked Halleck's apparent decisiveness. Had he finally found a general that he could count on?

Despite Halleck's insistence, however, McClellan would not budge. He insisted that he was right and was not going to risk his army. Instead of forcing McClellan to obey his order, Halleck started to equivocate and began to fret. In addition to McClellan, he faced serious problems in other theaters of the war. Don Carlos Buell was dragging his feet in the West, and guerrilla activity against U. S. Grant was increasing in north Mississippi. In Kansas, the eccentric Jim Lane was recruiting black soldiers, and Halleck thought this was totally inappropriate. Admiral David Farragut's attempt to take Vicksburg had failed. Lincoln wanted Halleck to fix these problems.

Halleck felt overwhelmed, and he lost sleep. He even worried that because Lincoln had given him everything he had asked for, the president would accept no excuses for failure. Halleck, the great administrator, was being asked to make recalcitrant and confusing individuals and events bend to his will. He agonized over what might go wrong instead of looking for opportunities to excel. The cabinet started to notice his anxiety. McClellan grew increasingly abrasive and insulting in his relationship with Halleck, and McClellan even told Lincoln that he was considering letting Pope "get out of his scrape" on his own. Halleck had lost control.[3]

Everything came crashing down in almost an instant. From August 28 to 30, 1862, Robert E. Lee and Stonewall Jackson smashed Pope's Army of Virginia at the Second Battle of Bull Run (Manassas) while McClellan's Army of the Potomac reluctantly moved toward that area. Halleck panicked. He blamed McClellan for Pope's defeat, but he still begged him, "Assist me in this crisis with your ability and experience. I am utterly tired out." Just a few days previously, Lincoln had said that McClellan was "a little crazy" with "envy, jealousy, and spite," while Halleck was only concerned that "the service is benefitted." Yet when Lincoln met with Halleck and McClellan on September 1 and 2, with Stanton conspicuously absent, the president asked McClellan to save Washington and perhaps the war effort itself. When the cabinet heard about this, Secretary of the Navy Gideon Welles said, "There was a more disturbed and desponding feeling than I have ever witnessed in council; the President was greatly distressed." Conversely, soldiers in the Army of the Potomac "danced and frolicked like schoolboys."[4]

Lincoln quickly took charge. He ordered Halleck to prepare a field army without weakening the force needed to protect Washington. Knowing that McClellan and Pope could not work together and that McClellan was enormously popular with the Army of the Potomac, Lincoln fired Pope and assigned him to sensitive non–Civil War duty, sending him to Minnesota to put down a dangerous Sioux Indian uprising. Meanwhile, Robert E. Lee and the Army of Northern Virginia began a movement into Maryland to try to bring that slave state into the Confederacy. McClellan followed Lee and had the good fortune to have some Union soldiers find a copy of Lee's battle orders wrapped around some cigars in an abandoned Confederate camp. He clashed with Lee at Antietam (Sharpsburg), a savage battle that saw a combined 22,700 casualties. Lee had to retreat into Virginia, and McClellan held the field, so by the standards of combat in that war, McClellan was the winner.[5]

Lincoln took advantage of this victory to deal with slavery's role in the war, the Constitution, and the nation. In July 1862, Congress had presented him with the Second Confiscation Act. He agreed with most of it, but he believed that the constitutional ban on "forfeiture . . . beyond the lives of the guilty parties" negated Congress's action, as did the lack of "a conviction of the supposed criminal." Congress quickly passed a revised law, this time without the sections Lincoln found constitutionally offensive, and he signed it.

This legislation was an important step toward emancipation. It was not, however, the first freeing of slaves in rebellious states, Ben Butler's contraband declaration and the First Confiscation Act of August 1861 had had that effect, but neither was really enforced. In the 1862 law, slaveholders had sixty days to surrender or lose their slaves. Importantly, too, this law told army officers that any slaves escaping to Union camps were to be freed. According to Lincoln's wish, moreover, graduated emancipation was now in the law. The federal government would compensate loyal slaveholders for freeing their slaves.[6]

Lincoln pushed even further. He read a memorandum during his July 22, 1862, cabinet meeting explaining that black people could be recruited into the army—free black men; slaves of rebellious owners; and slaves of loyal owners, but these only with the owners' consent. Slaves "not suitable for recruits" were not to be considered.[7] Lincoln's government had moved far along the road to emancipation. In the war, the concepts of union and emancipation were being intertwined.

At that same cabinet meeting, Lincoln also read a draft of what was to become the Emancipation Proclamation. He had been working on this statement in secret for a number of weeks and decided the time was ripe to make it public. The cabinet disagreed with him. Secretary of State William Henry Seward urged him not to release the document until Union armies could win an important military victory. If he issued it now, it would look like a gesture of desperation. Lincoln agreed and put the paper in his pocket.

With the Emancipation Proclamation still an unpromulgated secret, Lincoln instead issued a proclamation enforcing the July 17 Second Confiscation Act. He told "all persons . . . to cease participating in, aiding, countenancing, or abetting the exiting rebellion, or any rebellion against the government of the United States, to return to their proper allegiance to the United States, on pain of . . . forfeitures and seizures." These words were taken directly from the draft of the Emancipation Proclamation that Lincoln had read to his cabinet, and they indicated his determination to follow through on his emancipation plan.[8]

He gave another hint in answering a New York financier who had sent him a letter from "a very wealthy and influential planter" in Louisiana calling on the North to "say officially that it wishes for the restoration of the Union as it was." In a phrase, this planter wanted Lincoln to be willing to restore the Union with slavery intact. Carefully choosing his words, Lincoln replied, "Broken eggs cannot be mended, but Louisiana has nothing to do but to take her place in the Union as it was, barring the already broken eggs." Lincoln was hinting at the consequences if Louisiana did not move toward peace quickly. "These enemies must understand that they cannot experiment for ten years trying to destroy the government, and if they fail still come back into the Union unhurt." Under the Constitution, which Lincoln was fighting to defend, slavery was protected, he indicated, but that protection was obviously breaking down, and there was no guarantee it would not soon be totally lost.[9]

Yet slavery's existence was not eroding fast enough for everyone. On August 4, just two weeks after the cabinet meeting where he had talked about black soldiers, Lincoln responded negatively to a delegation from Indiana who came to see him with the "offer [of] two colored regiments." He immediately responded that he would employ black men in the army as laborers "but would not promise to make soldiers of them." He said he worried that if he did, it "would turn 50,000 bayonets from the loyal Border States against us that were for us."[10]

Two weeks later, on August 20, Horace Greeley put further pressure on Lincoln in an open letter in the *New York Tribune* titled "The Prayer of Twenty Millions." He called on the president to realize that it made no sense to be attempting "to put down the rebellion and at the same time uphold its inciting cause." There must be an end, Greeley said, to the "mistaken deference to Rebel Slavery." Here was a statement that was directly opposite to that sent by the Louisiana planter, and Lincoln had another chance to talk about the future of slavery, this time publicly.

On August 22, Lincoln told the reading public in one of Greeley's rival newspapers, "My paramount object in this struggle *is* to save the Union, and is *not* either to save or destroy slavery." And then, signifying more than the public could imagine at the time, he continued, "If I could save the Union without freeing *any* slave I would do it, and if I could save it by freeing *all* the slaves I would do it. . . . What I do about slavery and the colored race, I do because I believe it helps to save the Union."[11]

Although the public in those days, and even some historians later, read this statement as indicating that Lincoln really was not antislavery, in fact he was. He personally wanted to see the slaves set free, but officially, according to the Constitution, he could not do this except in the context of battling to save the Union. For the first time, however, he bluntly said that if he had to end slavery in order to preserve the Union, he would do so. Having already decided to issue the Emancipation Proclamation, Lincoln was displaying his craftiness. He was preparing the country for what was to come. He did the same thing in a message to Chicago Christians who were calling for immediate emancipation, telling them that were he to issue such a proclamation, it would "be inoperative, like the Pope's bull against the comet." Yet this did not mean that he believed there were legal or moral reasons against making such a statement. "As commander-in-chief of the army and navy, in time of war, I suppose I have a right to take any measure which may best subdue the enemy."[12]

The announcement of Lincoln's proclamation still awaited a Union military success. On September 22, 1862, news of McClellan's narrow victory at Antietam (Sharpsburg) arrived, and Lincoln wasted little time. He formally issued the Emancipation Proclamation, carefully fitting it into the Constitution's still existing protection of slavery. He issued the proclamation as a war measure, he said, part of the military effort to preserve the Union. He had said that he would attack slavery if he thought it necessary to preserve the Union, and now he did just that. The conservative war of preserving the Union became a revolutionary war to end slavery too. Lincoln had moved the nation a long way in less than a year and a half.[13]

He also suspended the writ of habeas corpus, saying that anyone "affording aid and comfort to Rebels against the authority of the United States shall be subject to martial law and liable to trial and punishment by Courts Martial or Military Commission."[14] This pronouncement, like the Emancipation Proclamation, revolutionized the war.

Yet George B. McClellan remained unwilling to go forward after Antietam. Lincoln kept pressing, but McClellan kept resisting, and Halleck had little to add. Lincoln told McClellan that he was "over-cautious" because he "assume[d]" he could "not do what the enemy [was] constantly doing." McClellan had written Halleck that he could not supply his army at Winchester unless a particular railroad was built, but Lincoln pointed out that the Confederates were surviving there at a much greater distance from a railroad line than he was. He reminded McClellan of "one of the standard maxims of war . . . 'to operate upon the enemy's communications as much as possible without exposing your own,'" and noted, "You seem to act as if this applies *against* you, but can not apply in your *favor.*" On and on, Lincoln pointed out the fallacy in McClellan's military thinking, demonstrating his increasingly superior understanding of the principles of nineteenth-century warfare.[15]

It was all to no avail. McClellan continued to insist that he needed more men, draft animals, and supplies. When he demanded more cavalry mounts because he had nothing but "sore-tongued and fatigued horses," Lincoln shot back, "Will you pardon me for asking what the horses of your army have done since the battle of Antietam that fatigues anything?" McClellan took affront, and a correspondence on horses ensued. Lincoln expressed his frustration at hearing "that the cavalry horses were too much fatiegued [*sic*] to move." This "presented a very cheerless, almost hopeless, prospect for the future," he told McClellan, "and it may have forced something of impatience into my despatches."[16]

Feeling so upset at McClellan, Lincoln looked for good news elsewhere. In the West, General William S. Rosencrans had won a hard-fought victory at Corinth on October 3–4, and Lincoln sent his commander, Ulysses S. Grant, heartfelt congratulations. And in Perryville, Kentucky, on October 8, Don Carlos Buell had defeated Confederate general Braxton Bragg. When Stanton gave orders to John A. McClernand to go to the Midwest and organize the drafted or volunteer soldiers there into an expedition against Vicksburg, Lincoln responded happily that he "felt deep interest in the success of the expedition, and desire[d] it to be pushed forward with all possible dispatch."[17]

McClellan's refusal to press his success at Antietam only increased the calls in Washington for Lincoln to fire him. Lincoln could not easily do so, however, as he had asked McClellan to save Washington. But Lincoln's cabinet was so determined that Lincoln relieve McClellan that on August 30, even before Antietam, Secretary of the Treasury Salmon Chase and Attorney General Edward Bates drew up separate letters against the general, which other secretaries, including Stanton, signed. At a meeting that same day, the president appeared "in deep distress." He said that he felt "almost ready to hang himself."[18] But he stuck with McClellan because there was no one else to take his place.

On November 5, 1862, Lincoln realized at last that he had to act, so he fired McClellan and replaced him with Ambrose Burnside. The Rhode Island general was hardly enthusiastic about his promotion and insisted that he was not qualified for it. Perhaps to gain some divine guidance for his new general, Lincoln acquiesced to the demand of religious leaders who visited him in the White House, issuing an order calling on the army and the nation to observe the Sabbath properly.[19] What the generals were not accomplishing, perhaps God would.

Lincoln held a meeting with Burnside to plan the new commanding general's movement on Richmond. Burnside insisted that the way to do it was to take his 110,000 men (no more than this because he could not use them) and cross the Rappahannock River "in the face of the enemy." He admitted that this scheme was "somewhat risky." Lincoln did not want Burnside to make any risky crossings, however, and he did not want him to do anything that would push the Confederates back into their Richmond entrenchments. Lincoln said he had a better plan. He wanted to accumulate a force of around

25,000 men on the south bank of the Rappahannock River, near Port Royal, with two gunboats providing protection. A similar force should gather "high up the Pamunkey" River, again protected by gunboats. These two units should move simultaneously, while Burnside's force crossed the Rappahannock River at Fredericksburg. "If Gen. B. succeeds in driving the enemy from Fredericksburg," he explained, "the enemy no longer has the road to Richmond, but we have it and can march into the city. Or, possibly, having forced the enemy from his line, we could move upon and destroy his army." Lincoln was confident that his "plan promise[d] the best results, with the least hazard," but both Burnside and Halleck rejected it. They said it would take the Pamunkey force too long to get into position. If Lincoln recognized any irony, he did not comment on it. Whereas Lincoln's plan would require a longer span of time to implement, Burnside, insisting he did not want any more troops, would be able to go on the attack quickly. If nothing else, at least Lincoln was no longer dealing with the stubborn slowness of McClellan.[20]

Meanwhile, Lincoln argued for something that he continued to insist could solve the problem of slavery and aid the war effort: "compensated emancipation." In his annual message to Congress in December 1862, he proposed an amendment to the Constitution. He called for every state to end slavery by 1900 and be compensated by the Federal government for their losses of revenue, saying, "All slaves who shall have enjoyed actual freedom by the chances of war, at any time before the end of the rebellion, shall be forever free; but all owners of such, who shall not have been disloyal, shall be compensated for them." And "free colored persons, with their own consent" could be colonized "at any place or places without the United States."

Lincoln clearly saw no future for slavery: "Without slavery the rebellion could never have existed; without slavery it could not continue." He concluded, "In *giving* freedom to the *slave*, we *assure* freedom to the *free*—honorable alike in what we give, and what we preserve. We shall nobly save, or meanly lose, the last best, hope of earth. Other means may succeed; this could not fail."[21] Lincoln forthrightly insisted that unless slavery's future was considered and determined, the war had no chance of success.

As 1862 ended, therefore, Lincoln's reaction to the successes and failures on the battlefield had created a more revolutionary approach to the war. He had said in his 1861 inaugural address that slavery would not be touched because the Constitution protected it. Yet it was now on the block for extinction. In the Emancipation Proclamation, Lincoln had argued that this manner of ending slavery was constitutional because it was the application of one of the president's war powers. In his annual message, he argued for a constitutional amendment to establish compensated emancipation and colonization. Success in the war, the restoration of the Union, now rested firmly on the pillars of emancipation. Lincoln was pressing the country to realize that there was no hope of national preservation without an end to human bondage.

"IT IS THE OLD DIFFICULTY"

On December 13, 1862, the new commander of the Army of the Potomac, Ambrose Burnside, sent his troops across the Rappahannock River against Confederates entrenched on Marye's Hill looking down on Fredericksburg, Virginia. Unlike George McClellan, Burnside did not hesitate. He attacked. The frontal charge proved a disaster. Lincoln was crushed again, but as always, he tried to maintain the army's optimism. He told its soldiers that what they had done during the battle showed that they "possess[ed] all the qualities of a great army, which will yet give victory to the cause of the country and of popular government."[1]

Two of Burnside's subordinate generals disagreed. They wrote Lincoln that Burnside's direct attack had never had any chance of success. They called for a different approach, which in reality was a repeat of the Peninsula Campaign tried by former commander George B. McClellan. Lincoln read the message and pointed out that neither approach was without problems. "It is the old difficulty," he said with a sigh.[2]

As 1863 dawned, therefore, the Army of the Potomac had been defeated again and was clearly split. Some of its generals still longed for McClellan, but Burnside was determined to repeat his attack across the Rappahannock. Lincoln turned to his commanding general, Henry W. Halleck, for advice. On January 1, he told Halleck that Burnside wanted to cross the Rappahannock River again but his so-called "Grand Division commanders" were opposed. Accustomed to Halleck's refusal to give advice in the past, Lincoln told his commanding general, "If in such a difficulty as this you do not help, you fail me precisely in the point for which I sought your assistance." Lincoln wanted Halleck to investigate Burnside's plan thoroughly, he said, and "then tell Gen. Burnside that you *do* approve, or that you do *not* approve his plan. Your military skill is useless to me, if you will not do this."[3]

Halleck was not to be pressured. He refused to give Lincoln his opinion on the battle plans of a subordinate general and immediately submitted his resignation. He had always believed, he said, that generals in the field should make decisions for their armies, and his job was only to advise. Now, however, he did not even want to give any advice. Even when Burnside asked for help, Halleck said no.

When he saw Halleck's response, Lincoln must have gasped. He resignedly wrote at the bottom of his original letter to Halleck, "Withdrawn, because considered harsh by Gen. Halleck." Lincoln was facing opposition and veritable rebellion in the leadership of the army, and although he unhappily spoke of "General Halleck's habitual attitude of demur" and found it exasperating, he did not fire either Halleck or Burnside. There was no one else to take Halleck's place, and Burnside seemed determined to press forward. In that sense, he was better than McClellan.[4]

That same New Year's Day, Lincoln and his wife held a traditional reception at the Executive Mansion, and a host of people passed through the receiving line, each shaking the president's hand. When the reception was over, Lincoln took a nation-changing step. He went upstairs and prepared to sign the Emancipation Proclamation, putting its provisions into force as he had promised the nation the previous September. As he tried to grip the pen, however, he noticed his hand was unsteady and realized that the tremor was the result of all his hand shaking at the reception. He decided to wait until the tremor ceased; he did not want to sign such a monumental document with an uncertain signature. He did not want anyone who looked at it in later years to think that it indicated any indecision on his part. Later that evening, when he did sign the Emancipation Proclamation, his hand was steady and his signature was firm and true.

This was certainly one of the most dramatic moments in the history of the United States. In the midst of fighting a difficult civil war replete with uncertainty, Abraham Lincoln had taken that conflict to a new level. As commander in chief, as a war president, he used his constitutional power to free the slaves in all those areas still in rebellion against the Union. In the document, he also authorized the use of black soldiers, "colored troops," as they came to be known. The war to preserve the Union was definitely now a war to end slavery.[5]

Lincoln linked union and emancipation in a message he sent to Union major general John A. Dix, the commander at Fortress Monroe. "The proclamation has been issued," he said. "We were not succeeding—at best, were progressing too slowly—without it." Lincoln said he knew some people did not like the idea of black troops, and Dix himself indicated that he did not trust black men as soldiers.[6]

Lincoln was not deterred, however. He urged Andrew Johnson, military governor of Tennessee, to favor the use of black troops; given his standing as "an eminent citizen of a slave-state, and himself a slaveholder," his support would be especially meaningful. "The bare sight of fifty thousand armed, and drilled black soldiers on the banks of the Mississippi, would end the rebellion at once," Lincoln insisted. "If you *have* been thinking of it please do not dismiss the thought."[7]

In the past, Lincoln had experienced major disagreements with Generals John C. Fremont and David Hunter about the power of military officers to free slaves, but he now congratulated Hunter on the performance of his black troops at Jacksonville, Florida. He warned the general to be very attentive, however, realizing the dangers inherent in including black soldiers in the Federal military. "The enemy will make extra efforts to destroy them; and we should do the same to preserve and increase them," Lincoln said. Using black troops aided the Union effort, but Lincoln also realized that it created new problems.[8]

While the nation mulled over the new document, neither Lincoln nor Halleck thought to reject Burnside's attack plan or come up with anything else to take its place. In mid-January 1863, therefore, Burnside attempted a flanking movement on the Confederate army through the rain-soaked Virginia countryside. He quickly became mired in the mud. This futile movement became known as the "Mud March," and Burnside became the butt of ridicule. Once again Burnside appealed to Halleck for help and advice, and once again Halleck refused to provide any. Upset and unsure what to do next, Burnside went to see the president on January 25.

Lincoln asked Stanton and Halleck to join them, but he quickly took control of the meeting. Burnside wanted to fire all his critical subordinates or he would resign himself. Without giving Stanton or Halleck a chance to say anything, Lincoln replaced Burnside with Joseph Hooker, one of the very subordinates Burnside had wanted to fire. Halleck was unhappy with Lincoln's decision because he and Hooker had clashed in 1850s California, and neither could stand the other. Yet Halleck did not offer a word of opposition. Once more, he did not provide Lincoln with the advice that the president so badly wanted.[9]

Lincoln did not hire Hooker with his eyes closed. He knew all about the general's reputation for womanizing and drinking and his behind-the-scenes activities to undercut Burnside when the latter commanded the Army of the Potomac. As he appointed Hooker, Lincoln handed him a letter that indicated that there were things about him that were bothersome. He recited Hooker's positive attributes, but then reminded the general how he had tried to undercut Burnside and said that this activity might come back to haunt him. Lincoln was particularly unhappy with Hooker's statement that "both the Army and the Government needed a Dictator." "Of course, it was not *for* this, but in spite of it, that I have given you the command. Only those generals who gain successes, can set up dictators. What I now ask of you is military success, and I will risk the dictatorship." Hooker accepted this letter surprisingly well; in fact, he told a reporter, "That is just such a letter that a father might write to his son."[10]

Knowing that Halleck and Hooker disliked each other, Lincoln also told Hooker that he did not have to report to Halleck; he could report directly to the president. This was a startling decision on Lincoln's part. He took Halleck, his commanding general, completely out of the chain of command, but he kept him on anyway. He still believed in Halleck's intellect and still hoped that the general would prove militarily effective.

When Lincoln had fired McClellan earlier in the fall and replaced him with Burnside, he also had fired Don Carlos Buell in the West and replaced him with William Rosecrans. Lincoln had relieved McClellan and Buell because of their inability or unwillingness to take the offensive, but their replacements proved inadequate too. Burnside tried but failed, whereas Rosecrans delayed and demanded more supplies, more of everything, before he could move. He sounded just like McClellan and Buell.

Halleck had tried to prod Rosecrans into action, threatening him with removal. Rosecrans merely scoffed at that threat. Not surprisingly, Halleck then backed off. Throughout his debate with Rosecrans, Halleck kept using Lincoln's name, not speaking on his own behalf. He said the president was "greatly dissatisfied" with Rosecrans's complaints and delays and had good reasons for wanting military movement in Rosecrans's region. He admitted, however, that Lincoln had "never told" him "what those reasons were."

Rosecrans delayed as long as he could, and then he fought Braxton Bragg's Confederates at Stones River (Murfreesboro), the fierce battle taking place from December 31, 1862, to January 2, 1863. Rosecrans lost thirteen thousand men and Bragg lost twelve thousand, but Rosecrans held his ground and forced Bragg to retreat. Rosecrans's victory was a bloody one, but Halleck called it "one of the most brilliant of the war." Lincoln was equally happy, writing Rosecrans, "God bless you, and all with you!"[11] Unlike Burnside's debacle at Fredericksburg at this same time, Rosecrans had produced a much-needed victory.

Unfortunately, Rosecrans did not follow up this success. He complained and he demanded, but he did not move. In mid-March, for example, Rosecrans argued that Stanton had promised after Stones River, "Anything you & your command want, you can have." He lacked everything, he said, and even his rank was inadequate. He really should outrank Grant, Rosecrans insisted, because he had been in the military longer than the other man. "The world will not forget that you fought the battle of 'Stone River' and it will never care a fig whether you rank Gen. Grant on paper, or he so, ranks you," Lincoln lectured Rosecrans in response. "Be assured, you wrong both yourself and us, when you even suspect there is not the best disposition on the part of us all here to oblige you."[12] The general that Lincoln had appointed to replace an earlier troublesome one was proving difficult as well.

In Grant's area along the Mississippi River, there was movement, but Lincoln had problems in that region too. Grant was planning the capture of Vicksburg, and it was Lincoln himself who placed this effort in jeopardy because of his support for longtime Springfield, Illinois, friend John A. McClernand. A Democratic Party member of the U.S. House of Representatives, McClernand convinced Lincoln that he could raise a large number of troops in his native southern Illinois, and that he could then lead this army to victory at Vicksburg. Lincoln had long hoped to control the Mississippi River, so he reacted enthusiastically to McClernand's idea. Not so Halleck, Grant, and Sherman, who were sure that McClernand would make a mess of what West Pointers like them could handle easily.

Henry Halleck, who had difficulty standing up to George B. McClellan, another West Point graduate, had no problem working around politician-turned-general John A. McClernand. He let Grant and Sherman know that as soon as the troops McClernand recruited arrived in Memphis, Grant would have complete control over them. Grant did not hesitate. Before McClernand could arrive, Grant quickly put into motion his own plan for capturing Vicksburg. He sent William T. Sherman down the river to attack the northern end of the Walnut Hills, upon which Vicksburg stood. As Sherman later characterized it, "The preparations [and departure] were necessarily hasty in the extreme." Grant was to move his army south by way of Grenada, Mississippi, and attack from east of Vicksburg. It was also hoped that Nathaniel P. Banks, then in Louisiana, would move north up the river to complete a three-pronged attack.

But Banks did not move north, and Grant's supply depot in Holly Springs came under the torch of Confederate general Earl Van Dorn. Sherman unknowingly was on his own. His men boarded

Commander David D. Porter's naval vessels, with Chickasaw Bayou standing as a watery barrier between the Federal men and the heavily entrenched Confederates. Sherman's December 27, 1862, attack proved a disaster. As he told his wife, "Well, we have been to Vicksburg and it was too much for us, and we have backed out." Adding to the disappointment, Sherman learned that McClernand had arrived and, by virtue of his seniority, had taken command of the expedition on January 2, 1863. Horrified at this development, Grant, who outranked McClernand, hurried downriver and took command away from him. Grant told Lincoln and Halleck, "I have not confidence in his ability as a soldier to conduct an expedition of the magnitude of this one successfully." He believed that all his officers felt the same way.[13]

The Illinois general became furious. He told Lincoln that he wanted Halleck charged "with willful contempt of superior authority" for disobeying Lincoln's and the secretary of war's expedition order. Lincoln had to have been surprised at the actions of his commanding general, but he stood by him. He answered McClernand's message firmly. "I have too many *family* controversies (so to speak) already on my hands, to voluntarily, or so long as I can avoid it, take up another. You are now doing well—well for the country and well for yourself—much better than you could possibly be if engaged in open war with Gen. Halleck."[14]

Lincoln demonstrated his support of Grant by expanding his operational command to include Arkansas. Grant now had control of both sides of the Mississippi River. Even an unfortunate attempt by Grant to deal with the aggressive merchants in his area did not permanently hurt his standing in Washington. Instead of ejecting troublesome merchants of all religious persuasions, Grant had ordered all Jews out of his area. Lincoln quickly revoked the order, correctly feeling that it was wrong to stigmatize an entire group the way Grant had unfairly labeled the Jews. It was an obvious faux pas, but Lincoln appreciated Grant's willingness to be militarily aggressive, and he let it go at that.[15]

At this same time, Lincoln had taken action in Louisiana. He sacked Benjamin Butler in December 1862 and replaced him with another political general, Nathaniel P. Banks. He told Banks that he still planned to have him head an independent expedition to Texas in order to send a message to the European powers in Mexico. Lincoln wanted him to begin that move as soon as his troops were no longer needed in the Mississippi Campaign.[16]

Lincoln's major interest in the West continued to be Vicksburg, however. He kept track of activities on the Mississippi River, noting, as did the country, that no real progress was being made. Lincoln favored a plan to dig a canal across the neck of land above Vicksburg, hoping that the river would flow into that canal and thus avoid Vicksburg, leaving it high and dry and allowing Union forces to pass it by. Union soldiers dug away, but the river refused to change its flow. Grant then tried getting to Vicksburg through a series of waterways, creeks, swamps, and bayous. Again, he had no success, but this activity kept his men busy while waiting for the wet, cold winter to turn into warmer spring.[17]

As spring arrived in the East, Joseph Hooker was busy getting the Army of the Potomac into psychological and fighting shape. During the winter, as was usually the case, the war ground to a halt, Burnside's Mud March giving credence to the validity of such a slowdown. Hooker was doing a good job of feeding his men and sheltering them well, and he was even granting furloughs so that many could visit their families. Throughout, Hooker communicated directly with the president, leaving Halleck out of the loop. Halleck did not appreciate such treatment, and he continued to send Hooker regular messages of advice, which were just as regularly ignored.

In late April 1863, Hooker began his movement against the Confederate army at Chancellorsville, making no effort to let Halleck know what he was doing. Hooker's plan called for a major flanking movement against the Confederate left. The attack seemed to be going well, but then Hooker lost his nerve and stopped the steady drive. Instead, he told his troops to dig in. Robert E. Lee audaciously split his force in the face of the enemy and sent Stonewall Jackson on a successful flanking movement against Hooker's unsecured right flank. Lee crossed the Federals' "T." Jackson rolled up the flank and sent Union soldiers fleeing, notably, O. O. Howard's XI Corps.

On other parts of the battlefield, however, the Federals were holding their own, and when Hooker called for a retreat, these soldiers could not understand why. In fact, Lee lost 21 percent of his whole army, while Hooker lost only 15 percent of his. But Lee still won an important victory.[18]

Lincoln had not known what was going on and told those around him that he "had a feverish anxiety to get facts." News did not arrive until May 6, and Lincoln became "extremely dejected." Once again, he faced a situation where his chosen general had failed him. The following day, Lincoln pointed out to Hooker that his offensive was completed "without effecting its object, except perhaps some important destruction of the enemy's communications," and asked, "What next?" Lincoln wanted a quick follow-through, but no matter what, he did not "wish anything done in desperation or rashness." Yet "an early movement would also help supersede the bad moral effect of the recent one, which is sure to be considerably injurious." Did Hooker have any plan? Lincoln asked. "If you have, prosecute it without interference from me. If you have not, please inform me, so that I, incompetent as I may be, can try [to] assist in the formation of some plan for the Army."[19] Lincoln said nothing about getting Halleck's advice.

On May 14, 1863, Lincoln once again expressed his disappointment to Hooker. He reminded the general that he had written to him previously, urging a renewed offensive because Lee's communications had been damaged and "he was somewhat in a deranged position." But "that idea has now passed away," Lincoln said, because the Confederate army had repaired its damages and had even been reinforced. "I therefore shall not complain, if you do no more, for a time, than to keep the enemy at bay, and out of other mischief by menaces and occasional cavalry raids, if practicable; and to put our own army in good condition again." Lincoln worried that Hooker's subordinates were "not giving [him] their entire confidence" and believed that the general had to get to the bottom of this problem before he tried anything else.[20]

There was no danger of Hooker going on the offensive. Just the day before Lincoln's letter, that general had written to the president,

"I know that you are impatient, and I know that I am, but my impatience must not be indulged at the expense of dearest interests."[21] With all his generals, it seemed, Lincoln could not expect any forward military progress unless he pushed for it himself, and writing to one of his generals that he would not find fault with him for standing still was a ticket to even more delay.

Fortunately for Lincoln's well-being, he received word just a week later that Ulysses S. Grant had defeated Confederate general John C. Pemberton at Champion Hill in Mississippi and had sent him fleeing across the Big Black River toward Vicksburg. The following day, Lincoln learned from General Stephen Hurlbut in Memphis that the news was even better than that. Grant was putting Vicksburg under siege, and the city was about to capitulate. Grant was yet again providing Lincoln with some rays of hope in the Union's more typical military darkness. But even here all was not perfect. Not only was General McClernand grousing about his position in the army, but he also alienated his military colleagues when he slowed the Union massing of troops at New Carthage, Louisiana, because his new wife was traveling on one of the boats "with her servants and baggage." He also held a military review for the visiting Illinois governor and fired a multiple-gun salute despite an order from Grant to "conserve ammunition." As a result, the secretary of war gave Grant explicit authority to fire McClernand if he so desired.[22]

Immediately after the Battle of Chancellorsville, Lincoln and Halleck had visited Hooker's headquarters. Worrying about how fragile Hooker's ego might be, Lincoln told him at that time that he did not blame him for the defeat. Hearing this, Hooker seemed to feel better. Lincoln then left Halleck behind to try to learn what had happened and what shape the army was in. Not surprisingly, Halleck told Lincoln that the defeat was all Hooker's fault and that "Fighting Joe" seemed on the verge of resigning. Halleck urged Lincoln to accept the resignation, but the president wanted to give Hooker one more chance.[23]

It was at this time that Lincoln received a strong letter from a leading Illinois politician and friend, antislavery congressman Isaac N. Arnold, calling for Halleck's—not Hooker's—dismissal. This letter represented the general attitude throughout the nation about "Old Brains"—that he was a terrible commanding officer. Arnold called on his friend Lincoln to fire Halleck because he had driven important generals out of the army: Fremont, Butler, and Sigel. Lincoln wrote a strong letter in response, defending his continued support of Halleck. He said that the general had driven no one out of the army; the generals Arnold mentioned had all left of their own accord, and Lincoln could see no way of bringing them back without hurting others.

Consider Grant, Lincoln told Arnold. Whether or not that general took Vicksburg, he had conducted "one of the most brilliant [campaigns] in the world." Look at his subordinate commanders, people like McClernand, Sherman, and the others. "You can scarcely name one of them that has not been constantly denounced and opposed by the same men who are now so anxious to get Halleck out, and Fremont & Butler & Sigel in," Lincoln pointed out. "Without claiming to be your superior," he concluded, "my position enables me to understand my duty in all these matters better than you possibly can, and I hope you do not yet doubt my integrity."[24]

As if such controversy were not enough, Lincoln was also having problems with generals in other places. In May 1863, he dismissed Samuel R. Curtis in Missouri because the general had taken on leadership of one of the state's political factions in opposition to the governor, who took the other. As Lincoln could not fire the governor, he fired the general, replacing him with John M. Schofield. "If both factions, or neither, shall abuse you," he advised Schofield, "you will probably be about right. Beware of being assailed by one, and praised by the other." As for Curtis, Lincoln tried to let him down easily. "With me," he said to Curtis, "the presumption is still in your favor that you are honest, capable, faithful, and patriotic."[25]

Then Ambrose Burnside telegraphed from Cincinnati, upset that Lincoln's cabinet did not approve of his arrest of Copperhead Clement L. Vallandigham. Lincoln carefully pointed out that what the cabinet meant was that they "regretted the necessity of arresting" anyone. Once the deed had been done, Lincoln told Burnside, all in the cabinet "were for seeing you through with it."[26]

Lincoln also worried about Grant's activities around Vicksburg. After the general's early successes, he seemed to have bogged down. Lincoln telegraphed him to learn whether he was "in communication with Gen. Banks." Was Banks moving closer to him or in the opposite direction? When he heard from General Daniel Butterfield, one of Hooker's subordinates, that a Richmond newspaper was announcing Grant's defeat at Vicksburg, Lincoln refused to believe the rumor. He had just heard from Vicksburg that Grant's troops were still investing the city. Still, such rumors were annoying.[27]

As much as all these problems bothered him, Lincoln's major concern remained Joseph Hooker and his handling of the Federal army in the wake of a rumored movement north by Robert E. Lee. Lincoln told Hooker that he had only one bit of advice to give him: if Lee decided to move on a path north of the Rappahannock River, Hooker should not move south of the river. "In one word, I would not take any risk of being entangled upon the river, like an ox jumped half over a fence, and liable to be torn by dogs, front and rear, without a fair chance to gore one way or kick the other." Hooker should stay on the same side of the river as Lee and fight the Confederates there, Lincoln said. Hooker had other ideas, however. If Lee moved north, Hooker wanted to circle behind him and take Richmond. Lincoln could not have disagreed more. "I think *Lee's* Army, and not *Richmond,* is your true objective point. If he comes towards the Upper Potomac, follow on his flank, and on the inside track, shortening your lines, whilst he lengthens his. Fight him when opportunity offers. If he stays where he is, fret him, and fret him."[28]

Lincoln once again turned to his commanding general to evaluate a subordinate's ideas, this time Hooker's. As always, Halleck refused to do so, although this time he was willing to opine that stopping Lee's invasion and not attacking Confederates entrenched near Richmond made the most sense. In fact, though, Halleck once again had refused to take a stand, and Hooker could do what he wished.[29]

Despite Halleck giving him that much freedom, Hooker still believed the commanding general was interfering with him and complained directly to Lincoln. "You have long been aware Mr. President," Hooker wrote, "that I have not enjoyed the confidence of the Major General Commanding the Army & I can assure you so long as this continues we may look in vain for success." Lincoln responded calmly, telling Hooker, "You state the case much too strongly." Halleck was upset at him only because he did not like the idea that Hooker was dealing directly with Lincoln and not through him as commanding general. "I do not think he withholds any support from you on account of it," Lincoln insisted.[30]

Telegrams clicked back and forth, and it was clear that Hooker and Halleck did not understand how they were going to wage the battle against Lee within the context of their own sour relationship. Finally, Lincoln had had enough. At ten o'clock at night on June 16, 1863, he told Hooker that "to remove all misunderstanding," he was placing him under Halleck's direct military control. "I shall direct him to give you orders, and you to obey them." Lincoln thought that would solve the misunderstanding, but such was not to be. Halleck almost immediately told Hooker, "You are in command of the Army of the Potomac and will make the particular dispositions as you deem proper."[31] Lincoln could have dismissed Halleck immediately, but once again, he did not know who could take his place.

The disagreement between Halleck and Hooker grew worse, each man blaming the other for the disagreement, while Lee continued his move north. Finally, Halleck told Hooker that he had to hold Harper's Ferry, but Hooker said that was a waste of manpower. He wanted to withdraw the ten thousand men guarding that site and merge them into the Army of the Potomac. Halleck's insistence was the last straw for Hooker. He told the commanding general that if he was forced to do what he knew he could not do, he would resign. Halleck, Secretary of War Stanton, and Lincoln all read this ultimatum, and Lincoln immediately fired Hooker and replaced him with George G. Meade, one of the corps commanders.[32] It was then June 28, and Lee's army was continuing to advance north.

Because Vicksburg was so far away from Washington, Lincoln knew less about what was going on there than he knew about Virginia. He accepted the good news of Grant's siege of Vicksburg quietly. Grant did not bother Lincoln with constant appeals for more soldiers or with regular complaints about Henry Halleck. He just kept moving forward, so Lincoln saw no need to bother him. Even when Grant fired Lincoln's friend John McClernand, Lincoln did not intervene.[33]

The two theaters of war came crashing together in early July. In Pennsylvania, Meade held off Lee's legions at Gettysburg and forced that army to retreat back to Virginia, having suffered horrendous losses. In Mississippi, Grant's siege proved successful, and the Confederates had to surrender an entire army and their last major bastion on the Mississippi River. With the fall of Port Hudson immediately after, the Federals gained complete control of the river.

Lincoln heard the news from his secretary of the navy and responded passionately, "I cannot, in words, tell you my joy over this result. It is great, Mr. Welles, it is great!" Lincoln then also announced the Confederate loss at Gettysburg with exuberant words of praise to God. "Now," he wrote to General Halleck, "if General Meade can complete his work, so gloriously prosecuted thus far, by the literal or substantial destruction of Lee's army, the rebellion will be over."[34]

Lincoln was pleased with the victories at Vicksburg and Gettysburg, but he realized that these were not enough. The Union army had to destroy the Confederate army before it could claim success. In the early days of 1861 and at the First Battle of Bull Run, capture of territory had been the only concern. Now the Confederate army and the slavery that upheld Southern society had to be destroyed in order for the Federals to win the war and save the Union.

Winfield Scott, America's leading early nineteenth-century military leader and Lincoln's first commanding general. Library of Congress.

Soldiers of the 26th New York Volunteer Regiment displaying typical Civil War troop formation. Library of Congress.

Abraham Lincoln visiting George B. McClellan at Antietam to encourage the general to become more aggressive. Library of Congress.

Secretary of War Edwin M. Stanton, Lincoln's most significant civilian appointment. Library of Congress.

Ambrose Burnside, who was named commanding general of the Army of the Potomac by Lincoln, but proved to be a military failure at Fredericksburg and during the "Mud March." Library of Congress.

The 1863 Battle of Gettysburg exemplified the horrific casualties resulting from Civil War battles. Library of Congress.

An unidentified African American soldier, one of nearly two hundred thousand black men who served in the Federal military. Library of Congress.

Ulysses S. Grant, a talented individual who understood the war the way Lincoln did. Lincoln appointed him commanding general in 1864. Ulysses S. Grant Association's Ulysses S. Grant Presidential Library, Mississippi State University.

William T. Sherman's capture of Atlanta, an event that moved Lincoln's reelection campaign from almost certain defeat to victory. Library of Congress.

City Point, Virginia, where Lincoln's boat landed when he visited Grant's headquarters in 1865. Library of Congress.

CHAPTER SIX

"HE IS MANAGING THE WAR"

The great Union victories in early July 1863 at Vicksburg and Gettysburg produced different results. At Vicksburg, Ulysses S. Grant captured the city and its defending army. No victory could have been more total. At Gettysburg, on the other hand, the Army of the Potomac under George G. Meade regained control of the city and the hills and ridges around it, but Lee's bloodied army retreated and was still potent. Meade's great victory was not as total as Grant's.

Lincoln realized the limits of Meade's victory. As late as July 11, he believed that his general was going to attack Lee's army with its back to the Potomac River and score "a brilliant success" by "inflict[ing] the Coup de grace upon the flying Rebels." Nothing happened. Always happy to cite Lincoln, Henry Halleck expressed the president's exasperation in a telegram to Meade: "The enemy should be pursued and cut up. . . . I need hardly say to you that the escape of Lee's army without another battle has created great dissatisfaction in the mind of the President."[1]

Meade's feelings were hurt. He believed that Lincoln's "censure" was so "undeserved" that he should resign immediately. Halleck insisted that his earlier telegram "was not intended as a censure, but as a stimulus to an active pursuit." It certainly was not "a sufficient cause" for resignation. Lincoln immediately reassured his affronted general: "I am very—*very*—grateful to you for the magnificent success you gave the cause of the country at Gettysburg; and I am sorry now to be the author of the slightest pain to you." But, Lincoln said, he had been upset that Meade's Army of the Potomac was "not seeking a collision with the enemy," but was "trying to get him across the river without another battle." He concluded, "I do not believe you appreciate the magnitude of the misfortune involved in Lee's escape. . . . Your golden opportunity is gone, and I am distressed immeasureably [*sic*] because of it." Lincoln laid down his pen, but then quickly picked it up again and wrote on the letter's envelope, "To Gen. Meade, never sent, or signed."[2]

What especially upset Lincoln was the message Meade had crafted to his soldiers immediately after the battle. He had told them, "Our task is not yet accomplished, and the commanding general looks to the army for greater efforts to drive from our soil every vestige of the presence of the invader." Reading this statement, Lincoln expressed his dismay to Halleck. "This is a dreadful reminiscence of McClellan," he said. After Lee had retreated from Antietam, McClellan had said the same thing. "Will our Generals never get that idea out of their heads? The whole country is *our* soil."[3]

Feeling exasperated with Meade for his comment and his seeming refusal to engage Lee, Lincoln told his son, Robert, "If I had gone up there I could have whipped them myself." The president who began the war feeling militarily inferior to his generals now was so exasperated with them that he was ready to take the field himself.[4]

Perhaps the one thing that kept Lincoln from excoriating Meade even more was his satisfaction with Ulysses S. Grant. He wrote the western general a letter that said the complete opposite to what he had written to Meade. He told Grant that although they had almost certainly never met, he wanted to send "a grateful acknowledgment for the almost inestimable service you have done the country." He explained that throughout the Vicksburg Campaign, he had disagreed with and worried about Grant's movements. But "I now wish to make the personal acknowledgment that you were right, and I was wrong." According to William T. Sherman, when a group of ministers came to visit Lincoln to complain about what they believed inaccurately was "Grant's habit" of drinking too much, Lincoln listened carefully and then responded, "Do you know where Grant buys his whiskey? I would like to present some to other Generals not so successful."[5]

At this same time, Lincoln worked to include black soldiers in Union armies so as to help strengthen the Federal effort, particularly in the West. He told Secretary of War Edwin Stanton that he wanted "a renewed and vigorous effort . . . to raise colored forces along the shores of the Missisippi [*sic*]," and he issued an order vowing equal protection for black soldiers murdered or enslaved by the Confederates. For each one so treated, he promised that "a rebel soldier shall be executed" or "a rebel soldier shall be placed at hard labor on the public works." This so-called "Order of Retaliation" was published as General Orders No. 252, but it was never enforced.[6]

Lincoln was also happy with Nathaniel P. Banks, the head of Union military activity in the lower Mississippi River Valley, for his success at Port Hudson and the opening of the Mississippi River to total Union control. But he wanted Banks to do more. "Recent events in Mexico, I think, render early action in Texas more important than ever," he said. And Lincoln expressed his determination to proceed with emancipation. He hoped that Louisiana, which Banks supervised, would "make a new Constitution recognizing the emancipation proclamation, and adopting emancipation in those parts of the state to which the proclamation does not apply." He also desired a new relationship between black and white, including "education for young blacks." He called himself "an anti-slavery man" and said, "For my part I think I shall not, in any event, retract the emancipation proclamation; nor, as executive, ever return to slavery any person who is free by the terms of that proclamation, or by any of the acts of Congress."[7] Lincoln never allowed slavery to drift far from the war effort.

Feeling as strongly as he did about sending troops into Texas, Lincoln told Grant that his idea of capturing Mobile would have to be delayed until the Texas Expedition had been successfully completed. "I am greatly impressed with the importance of re-establishing the national authority in Western Texas as soon as possible," Lincoln said. He also believed that it was important to recruit black troops in Grant's area of command, noting that "it works doubly, weakening the enemy and strengthening us." "The emancipation proclamation has helped some in our military operations," said Grant. "By arming the negro we have added a powerful ally." As for Texas, he told Lincoln that he favored the idea of moving on Mobile, but he saw "the importance of a movement into Texas just at this time."[8] Grant did not bother Lincoln with this idea again, and Lincoln had to have noticed how differently Grant behaved compared with his other generals. Grant was willing to follow orders and do so without complaint. And he was winning battles.

Lincoln's continued attempts to push his generals into action often resulted in charges of interference. Secretary John Hay told a newspaper reporter friend who made such an accusation that if Lincoln "had kept his fingers from meddling with the war, we should now have had neither war nor government I think." He no longer questioned Lincoln, Hay said, because the president was always right. "I believe he will fill a bigger place in history than he even dreams of himself." Later Hay said of Lincoln, "He is managing the war, the draft, foreign relations, and planning a reconstruction of the Union, all at once." At that time, not many people agreed with Hay's praise.[9]

In fact, Lincoln addressed his legacy when he boldly responded to an invitation to attend a gathering of conditional Unionists in his home state of Illinois. He could not leave his duties in Washington, he said, but he appreciated the support of these longtime political friends. Wasting no time, however, he quickly addressed "those who are dissatisfied with me" because there was no peace in the nation. "To be plain, you are dissatisfied with me about the negro," he asserted. "You dislike the emancipation proclamation. . . . You say it is unconstitutional—I think differently. I think the constitution invests its commander-in-chief, with the law of war, in time of war." These included the right to confiscate property, and slaves were property. "You say you will not fight to free negroes," Lincoln continued. "Fight you, then, exclusively to save the Union." The addition of black troops provided help for the nation to do just that. Once victory comes, Lincoln said, "there will be some black men who can remember that, with silent tongue, and clenched teeth, and steady eye, and well-poised bayonet, they have helped mankind on to this great consummation; while, I fear, there will be some white ones, unable to forget that, with malignant heart, and deceitful speech, they have strove to hinder it."[10]

As he wrote these unflinching words, Lincoln must have been thinking of the heroic assault of the 54th Massachusetts Volunteer Infantry at the Second Battle of Fort Wagner, South Carolina, on July 18, 1863. This 600-man colored troop unit suffered 272 casualties and demonstrated the incredible bravery of black soldiers in combat. The nation and the army began to view black soldiers in a more positive light. Andrew Johnson, the military governor of Tennessee, even came out in favor of immediate emancipation in September, and Lincoln could not have been happier. "I see that you have declared in favor of emancipation in Tennessee, for which, may God bless you," he said.[11] Lincoln's view of the connection between union and emancipation and his belief that the war could not be won and the Union restored without an end to slavery and the use of black troops were starting to take hold in the nation.

But the war's results were still uncertain. George G. Meade and Robert E. Lee were at a stalemate in Virginia. In the West, William Rosecrans continued arguing about his need for more men and supplies. Commanding General Henry W. Halleck kept urging Rosecrans to take the offensive, but Rosecrans refused, telling Halleck—and thereby Lincoln—that if they only had "a true military appreciation of the advantages of not moving prematurely," they would not bother him so much. Halleck was furious at such an insult and said so: "In other words, general, while I am blamed here for not urging you forward more rapidly, you are displeased at my doing so."[12]

Surprisingly, Rosecrans masterfully maneuvered Bragg's army out of Chattanooga in early September 1863. The Confederate leaders in Richmond had already rushed James Longstreet to Tennessee to buttress Bragg, while Federal leaders in Washington talked of sending Grant and Sherman from Vicksburg and Burnside from Knoxville to reinforce Rosecrans. At the same time, Lincoln, Stanton, and Halleck changed their attitude toward Meade in Virginia. Because of the dangerous military activity elsewhere, they decided that they did not want Meade to begin any offensive. Lincoln remained concerned about the safety of Washington, but now he saw the West as crucial, perhaps the key to Union victory.[13]

On September 19–20, 1863, Bragg's Confederates attacked Rosecrans's Federals along Chickamauga Creek in Georgia, just south of Chattanooga. A mistake in command communication caused a gap in the Union line, just as Longstreet, newly arrived from Virginia, was attacking. The Confederates were able to rush through the gap and put the Federals to rout. Portions of the Union army with Rosecrans among them ran into Chattanooga. Were it not for General George H. Thomas stubbornly holding off the charging Confederates, earning himself the nickname "Rock of Chickamauga," the Confederates would have dealt the Union cause in the West an annihilating blow.[14]

The drubbing at Chickamauga Creek was a huge disappointment, which Lincoln felt severely in Washington, because early favorable news had lulled him into a false euphoria. On September 19, Lincoln had received a dispatch from Rosecrans "promising a complete victory on the next day." The following morning, however, John Hay was still asleep when Lincoln came into his room, crestfallen. He sat down on Hay's bed. "Well, Rosecrans has been whipped," Lincoln said sadly. Adding to his sorrow, he learned that his brother-in-law Benjamin H. Helm, a Confederate officer, had died in the battle. Helm's wife, Emily, was Mary Lincoln's half-sister and visited the White House after her husband's death. Lincoln defended her presence, despite public outrage.

Over the next several days, though, as more information came in, things looked better to Lincoln. George H. Thomas had indeed been a rock, and the fragmented Union army had seemingly come together in Chattanooga under Rosecrans.[15] The Federals still held the city, and from the perspective of Washington, that was crucial.

Lincoln believed that Rosecrans had to hold fast in Chattanooga because control of that city kept the Confederates in Tennessee at bay and broke a major Confederate railroad line. To make sure Rosecrans maintained his optimism and thus his will to fight, Lincoln wrote him a strong letter. "Be of good cheer. We have unabated confidence in you, and in your soldiers and officers," he said. "In the main you must be the judge as to what is to be done." When a day passed without any word from the general, however, Lincoln displayed his true emotions. "Please relieve my anxiety," he wrote to Rosecrans.[16]

Secretary of War Edwin M. Stanton realized that something besides cheering up had to be done to help Rosecrans in Chattanooga, so he called an emergency meeting of Lincoln's cabinet. The debate centered on whether Burnside should indeed be ordered to Chattanooga from Knoxville or Sherman should be sent there from Vicksburg. Stanton said that Joseph Hooker should go west by rail with the twenty thousand men of the XI and XII Corps, insisting that such a trip from Washington would take only around seven days. Lincoln, joined by Halleck, protested that it would take much longer than that; Halleck estimated that it would require several weeks. Stanton called the commander of the military railroad into the meeting and asked him how long such a trip would take. About seven days, General D. C. McCullum replied, and Stanton grew ecstatic that he had been correct. Hooker and his force left on September 25 and arrived in Chattanooga exactly seven days later.

Lincoln followed this reinforcement with a military consolidation in the region. He made Ulysses S. Grant commander of the entire western theater and ordered William T. Sherman to take Grant's place as commander of the Army of the Tennessee. Speaking through General Halleck, Lincoln gave Grant permission to either fire Rosecrans or keep him on. Grant, who had never thought much of Rosecrans, quickly fired him, appointing George H. Thomas to be the new commander of the Army of the Cumberland.[17]

Lincoln also ordered Grant and Sherman to Chattanooga to take command of the besieged Union army there. Sherman quickly got his new command moving. "With Grant, I will undertake anything in reason," he said. Sherman drove his men hard the six hundred miles from Vicksburg to Chattanooga, arriving some thirty miles from the Tennessee River city on November 13, 1863, and entering two days later to confer with Grant.[18]

Sherman, Thomas, and Hooker agreed on Grant's battle plan, which called for Hooker to take Lookout Mountain on the right, Thomas to handle the center, and Sherman to lead the way by attacking the Confederates on the left. Hooker was successful, but Sherman was stymied. Grant then ordered Thomas's men, in the middle, to capture the rifle trenches at the foot of Missionary Ridge.

When the soldiers reached the trenches, they did not stop. Without any command from their generals, they charged up the ridge and overwhelmed Bragg's Confederates on the top. The shocked Southern soldiers broke and ran. The siege of Chattanooga was over, and Union control of the city was ensured. It was not a total victory, because Bragg's army escaped to fight another day, but Lincoln was satisfied. On December 8, he congratulated Ulysses S. Grant and all his men for the Chattanooga victory, saying, "I wish to tender you, and all under your command, my more than thanks, my profoundest gratitude."[19]

Now that the Federals had won an important victory at Chattanooga in the West, Lincoln once again looked to Meade to do something in Virginia. He told Halleck that he thought Meade "should move upon Lee at once in manner of general attack, leaving to developments, whether he will make it a real attack." Such an offensive would give Meade better insight into Lee's plans than would cavalry probing. As he almost always did, however, Lincoln then caught himself. "Of course my opinion is not to control you and Gen. Meade," he assured Halleck.[20]

Lincoln clearly tried to leave matters to Meade, but he did not like that general's inaction. He bluntly told Halleck, "If the enemies sixty thousand are sufficient to keep our ninety thousand away from Richmond, why, by the same rule, may not forty thousand of ours keep their sixty thousand away from Washington, leaving us fifty thousand to put to some other use." Even that was beside the point, Lincoln continued. "My last attempt upon Richmond was to get McClellan, when he was nearer there than the enemy was, to run in ahead of him. Since then I have constantly desired the Army of the Potomac, to make Lee's army, and not Richmond, it's [*sic*] objective point."[21]

Lincoln also continued to have political problems in Missouri. He had appointed John M. Schofield there in the hope that he could bring a modicum of peace and understanding to the state. Like all his predecessors, however, Schofield found himself sucked into the seemingly never-ending political fray. Lincoln reacted by sending a letter to Schofield, copying it to some irate Missourians who had visited the president. In it, he set down some no-nonsense regulations. He told Schofield that his job was "to compel the excited people there to leave one another alone" and that he should arrest only those doing "*palpable* injury to the Military." No soldier or civilian should "be engaged in either returning fugitive slaves, or in forcing, or enticing slaves from their home" and "no one [was] to enlist colored troops" or "assume the functions of confiscating property." Basically, Lincoln wanted Schofield's military force to "expel guerrillas, marauders, and murderers, and all who are known to harbor, aid, or abet them," but "unauthorized individuals [were not] to perform the same service."[22] Thus even in one of the loyal states, albeit one still grappling with slavery, Lincoln had no peace.

Realizing that many Union soldiers were completing their terms of service, Lincoln also had to deal with a manpower problem. He had to issue another call for troops. He wanted three hundred thousand volunteers, over and above "the men raised by the present draft." Should a state fail to raise its quota, then a draft would be established in that state to make up the "deficiency."[23] Many governors were unhappy with this pronouncement, but Lincoln stood firm. He needed more soldiers, and he was determined to get them.

Lincoln also continued his study of military technology in the hope of boosting the Union war effort. He regularly test-fired weapons recommended to him, mostly in the Navy Yard, but sometimes he could be seen firing an exotic weapon on the White House lawn. During the hectic fall of 1863, Lincoln seemingly used this activity as a relaxation from the pressures of leadership. At the beginning of November, for example, he completed discussions with an inventor of a new kind of gunpowder and sent samples to a board consisting of military officers, skilled civilians, or both. Along with the powder, he sent the board a long set of detailed questions, including "Does it make less smoke?" "In proportion to effect produced, is it cheaper than common gun-powder?" and "Is it's [*sic*] manufacture simple, requiring no complicated apparatus, and is it attended with less danger than the manufacture of ordinary gun-powder?" On December 26, either taking the board's recommendation or making his own decision, Lincoln told the inventor that the government was not interested in his gunpowder.[24]

What proved to be the most important activity Lincoln conducted during this period was a planned trip to Gettysburg, Pennsylvania, for the dedication of a cemetery for the fallen Union soldiers of the July battle there. The night before the ceremony, a crowd in Gettysburg called on Lincoln at his hotel to make a speech. He declined to do so "for several substantial reasons," he said. "The most substantial of these is that I have no speech to make. [Laughter] In my position it is somewhat important that I should not say any foolish things."[25] The people had to wait until the next day to hear their president.

Lincoln did not say anything foolish. Well prepared, he gave the Gettysburg Address, one of the nation's most powerful orations. He took the war that he had been trying so hard to manage, the dedication of the cemetery, and the fallen soldiers being memorialized, and he consecrated them all. From that point on, there could be no doubt that the war was a conflict for freedom. The Union under fire was not the old Union of slavery, but the new Union of liberty. Lincoln's aim in the war became clear to anyone who pondered the words he said. Union and liberty were inseparable.[26]

Not always mentioned in the context of this magnificent speech are words that Lincoln wrote into his annual message to Congress less than three weeks after the Gettysburg Address: "The policy of emancipation, and of employing black soldiers, gave to the future a new aspect, about which hope, and fear, and doubt contended in uncertain conflict." But, he said, the nation was looking not just to a successful completion of the war, but to the reunification of all the states into a nation of liberty. In this vein, Lincoln issued his Proclamation of Amnesty and Reconstruction. Once 10 percent of a state's voters who had cast ballots in the 1860 presidential election took the oath of allegiance to the United States and reestablished a republican state government, their seceded state would be welcomed back into its proper relationship in the nation. Less than a month after his speech at Gettysburg, Lincoln rededicated the war as a fight for a renewed Union of all the states and all the peoples, black and white. He moved the nation yet again toward the belief that "this nation, under God, shall have a new birth of freedom."[27]

Lincoln was clearly determined to let the nation know that he would keep his promise to the slaves, who had long endured a life of degradation. Responding to a Massachusetts Anti-Slavery Society agent's request for an autograph, Lincoln wrote along with his signature, "I shall not attempt to retract or modify the emancipation proclamation, nor shall I return to slavery any person who is free by the terms of that proclamation, or by any of the acts of Congress."[28]

He also told James S. Wadsworth, a brigadier general who had been inspecting the United States Colored Troops whom General Lorenzo Thomas was recruiting in the Mississippi valley, what he wanted for black people in a reconstructed United States. This comment lacked the grandeur of the Gettysburg Address, but it concretely described Lincoln's thoughts about implementing those words. Black soldiers had "demonstrated in blood their right to the ballot," he said, concluding, "The restoration of the Rebel States to the Union must rest upon the principle of civil and political equality of both races; and it must be sealed by general amnesty."[29]

And thus, one year after he signed the final Emancipation Proclamation, and following a year of continued horrendous warfare, Lincoln insisted that the war would have to result in freedom and political equality for black people and amnesty for Southern whites. Blacks had proven their worth by their heroic role in combat. Southern whites now had to prove their loyalty to a reconstructed Union by swearing allegiance to the Constitution that Lincoln was trying to protect and to a society of free people, both black and white, that he led. This war, which had begun as a conflict to preserve the Union, had become a battle to end slavery, which, after all, had caused the war in the first place.

CHAPTER SEVEN

"HE HAS THE *GRIT* OF A BULLDOG!"

In early January 1864, Lincoln took another step, hardly as well known as the Emancipation Proclamation, but one that demonstrated that the war had changed. In 1861, Federal troops had captured Arlington, Virginia, just across the Potomac River from Washington. The home of Robert E. Lee was located there. Despite the Federal seizure, it remained legally in Lee family hands, although Mrs. Lee spent most of the war in Richmond.

In June 1862, Congress passed, and Lincoln signed, a law calling "for the collection of Direct Taxes in insurrectionary districts." On September 15, 1863, the Board of Tax Commissioners, following that law, set a tax of $92.07 on the eleven-hundred-acre, $34,000 Lee property. After the tax was not paid as required, this nonpayment was advertised in a local newspaper, and the property was put up for sale. When no offers were forthcoming, the property went to the United States, with Lincoln signing the January 1864 order. Thus the president of the United States confiscated the property of the leading general of the insurgent forces, indicating in the strongest manner possible that battling the Union had permanent repercussions.[1]

A series of letters about the same time between Lincoln and the governor of Kentucky also indicated the war's change. When the conflict began, Kentuckians had insisted on neutrality, but now, in January 1864, Governor Thomas E. Bramlette demanded that Lincoln countermand a Union army order sending troops away from Kentucky to Knoxville. He said this action put Kentucky in danger of "ruin." Lincoln responded that Grant had no doubt issued that order, and "Gen. Grant's judgment would be the highest incentive" for him to be supportive. That stopped Bramlette in his tracks. "If this order was with the approbation of Genl Grant," he said, "I will await the denouement before I venture a judgment of condemnation."[2]

Lincoln's hopes for a solution to the slavery matter also received official approval during this same period. Answering an attorney representing plantation owners about whether they could make work contracts with freed people to restart production of cotton, Lincoln responded, "I should regard such cases with great favor." Clearly Lincoln saw such economic activity as helping solve the problem of the future for the former slaves. This idea of establishing work contracts for newly freed slaves came at the right time, because an experiment to establish an all-black colony on the island of Vache, off the coast of modern-day Haiti, had failed. Lincoln was just then sending a ship to bring back colonists wishing to return.[3]

The problem of what role former slaves now residing in free states should play in the army and in the nation also was an issue. Massachusetts governor John A. Andrew wanted to keep black labor in his state, so he hoped to meet his state's draft quota by recruiting former slaves in the Southern states. Lincoln realized what Andrew was up to, and he facetiously asked him whether it was accurate "that Massachusetts wishes to afford a permanent home within her borders, for all, or even a large number of colored persons who will come to her." If this were the case, "I shall be only too glad to know it," he said. "It would give relief in a very difficult point."[4] This was not what Andrews had in mind, but Lincoln supported his plan to recruit in the South anyway.

Because 1864 was a presidential election year, political maneuvering had already begun. The difficult war situation made Lincoln's reelection problematic, and having to run under unfavorable conditions further complicated his life. A major problem even developed inside the cabinet. Samuel C. Pomeroy, senator from Kansas, served as the front man for Secretary of the Treasury Salmon P. Chase's attempt to replace Abraham Lincoln in the Executive Mansion. This movement was supposed to be secret, but it leaked out in late February 1864 in the form of a pamphlet soon called the Pomeroy Circular. Chase found himself in a difficult situation. He told Lincoln that he had never been aware of any letter of support for his candidacy until one appeared in a newspaper. A group of his friends had earlier approached him about the possibility of running for president, he said, but he had refused because he did not want to do anything to disrupt his work in the Treasury Department. His friends had disagreed, so he allowed them to go ahead, but he had stated emphatically that he would "render them no help." Since that time, he insisted, he had not met with anyone regarding the question. "For yourself," he declared, "I cherish sincere respect and esteem; and, permit me to add, affection." Chase expressed a willingness to resign if Lincoln thought this situation would create problems for him and his administration. Unfortunately for Chase, the true author of the circular, newsman James M. Winchell, insisted that Chase had known all along what was going on and had approved.[5]

Initially, Lincoln sent only a brief response. "I will answer a little more fully when I can find the leisure to do so," he said. A week later, Lincoln responded in detail, telling the secretary that he had known all along about this Chase boom for president. "Whether you shall remain at the head of the Treasury Department is a question which I will not allow myself to consider from any stand-point other than my judgment of the public service," Lincoln said, "and, in that view, I do not perceive occasion for a change."[6]

Upset because his public image had suffered, Chase sent newsman Henry Villard to see Lincoln to ask for the publication of all the correspondence between the two of them if the president approved. Lincoln turned him down. "In fact, [I] rather prefer to avoid an unnecessary exhibition," the president said. Then he cleverly lobbed it back to Chase: "You are at liberty, without in the least offending me, to allow the publication, if you choose." Three days later, on March 7, 1864, the *New York Herald* published Villard's story, which exonerated Chase and Lincoln of any wrongdoing. In truth, however, Lincoln once more was a political winner. He had put a recalcitrant cabinet member under control.[7]

Meanwhile, Halleck continued to be unpopular in Washington, but there were still many questions about Grant's fitness to replace him. Secretary of War Stanton sent his assistant, the former newsman Charles A. Dana, to visit Grant, as he had earlier done at Vicksburg. Dana reported back highly favorable information, and the difficult-to-please Stanton was happy with what he heard. Lincoln continued to be impressed with Grant, and Congress grew so impatient with Halleck that it pushed hard for Grant's promotion. On February 29, Lincoln nominated Grant to the rank of lieutenant general.[8] Only George Washington had ever held that high office before, so if Grant were promoted, he would outrank Halleck. (Winfield Scott had also been a lieutenant general, but only by an 1857 brevet.)

The hearings on this promotion proved so anti-Halleck that his friends tried to make sure that he did not suffer unduly from the process. Lincoln was less concerned with Halleck than he was with the possibility that Grant would become his political rival. Once he learned that Grant had no interest in the 1864 presidency, he too thought Grant was the man to command the Federal army. Through Stanton, he had Halleck call Grant to Washington.[9]

Grant arrived at the White House in the middle of a presidential reception on March 8, 1864. Lincoln was pleased to meet this general who had given him so much satisfaction. When he named Grant to be commanding general in place of Halleck, he created a new office for "Old Brains": chief of staff. Grant would make his headquarters with the Army of the Potomac, while Halleck stayed in Washington and, along with Stanton, took care of logistics and paperwork. Whether it was Lincoln or Stanton who came up with this idea, it proved to be an inspired one. It was the beginning of a modern command structure, with Lincoln as commander in chief, Grant as commanding general, and Halleck as chief of staff.

Lincoln had thus established a new military leadership team: Grant and Halleck, with Sherman the main subordinate in command of the West. Rumors spread that Halleck would refuse to cooperate with Grant out of spite, and one of Lincoln's secretaries even insisted that "Halleck is badly bilious about Grant." Lincoln was relieved when Halleck proved to be more than content with the new arrangement. He was extremely happy to be taking care of administration and offering advice rather than issuing orders. Sherman wished that Grant would stay in the West, but he took on his new post there with enthusiasm and a head full of ideas. As was typical, Grant displayed little emotion.[10]

Lincoln wanted Grant to take initiative and not be as unmovable and demanding as earlier generals. Lincoln did not give up political control over the war, but he did not want to make tactical decisions. He wanted Grant to do that, and while he would give him all the freedom of action he could, he wanted to know what was happening. Whether he knew that Grant shared his own admiration for Mexican War general Zachary Taylor is unclear. In 1850, Lincoln had eulogized Taylor as someone who "was never beaten and never retreated." Those were the characteristics he hoped Grant possessed too. Lincoln asked only two things of Grant. When the new commanding general accepted his commission, Lincoln wanted him to say something that would prevent other generals from getting jealous, and he wanted him to speak words that the Army of the Potomac would particularly want to hear. As he always did, however, Lincoln indicated that if Grant did not like anything Lincoln had suggested, he was free to do it his own way. As Grant was to do regularly in his new position, he followed Lincoln's advice.[11]

To demonstrate his support for his new military organization, Lincoln issued an order in mid-March 1864 extending the draft for another two hundred thousand men, "in addition to the five hundred thousand men called for February 1st, 1864." He gave each political entity until April 15 to raise volunteers to fill its quota, after which time the draft would begin. "There can be no army without men," he had written in September 1863 in a memorandum to himself. "Men can be had only voluntarily, or involuntarily. We have ceased to obtain them voluntarily; and to obtain them involuntarily, is the draft—the conscription."[12] Lincoln was determined to enlist the men his new generals needed to defeat secession.

Yet Lincoln had not solved all his military problems by appointing this new leadership team. Carl Schurz, political leader of the sizable German population in the North, wanted to continue in the military, but he also wanted to participate in the forthcoming presidential and congressional election. Lincoln said no. "I perceive no objection to your making a political speech when you are where one is to be made; but quite surely speaking in the North, and fighting in the South, at the same time, are not possible. Nor could I be justified," Lincoln insisted, "to detail any officer to the political campaign during its continuance, and then return him to the Army."[13]

Other military leaders also caused problems for Lincoln. Despite General David Hunter's controversial May 1862 emancipation edict, which resulted in his being relegated to Washington for a year on administrative duties, Lincoln ordered him to the Shenandoah Valley on May 21, 1864. Unfortunately, Hunter failed there and lost his post to Philip Sheridan. George Meade was upset that newspapers were full of denunciations of his performance at Gettysburg, and he blamed one of his subordinates, Daniel Sickles, for such bad press. He demanded a court of inquiry, which Lincoln immediately refused, telling Meade that neither his "honor" nor the "public interest" required an inquiry. The public was happy with his service, he said, and "agrees with me that it is much better for you [to] be engaged in trying to do more, than to be diverted, as you necessarily would be, by a Court of Inquiry."[14]

A recurring problem with Ohio colonel Thomas Worthington also upset Lincoln. Since Shiloh, Worthington had been attacking William T. Sherman and other military men for their alleged incompetence. When Worthington appealed to Lincoln, the president had no patience with him, penning a memorandum that demonstrated his disdain. "Today I verbally told Colonel Worthington that I did not think him fit for a Colonel," he said; "and now, upon his *urgent* request, I put it in writing."[15]

As much difficulty as such military matters caused Lincoln, they could not match what happened in Tennessee: the April 1864 massacre of black troops and white Unionists at Fort Pillow. Lincoln had long since decided that the Civil War had to result in freedom for the slaves and that black soldiers had to be included in the Federal army. His attempts to establish graduated emancipation and colonization were part of this effort, as was his establishment of the United States Colored Troops. The longer the war went on, the more Americans, North and South, realized that slavery was at the heart of it all. Whether or not they owned slaves themselves, Confederate soldiers inflicted a variety of outrages when they came in contact with black soldiers in blue uniforms. Lincoln understood this well and insisted that black troops be protected and treated in the same way that white soldiers were. It did not work that way, however, because Confederates often killed captured black soldiers along with their white officers and NCOs. Another frequent Confederate practice was to send black soldiers or civilians back into slavery.

It all came to a head in an out-of-the way place along the Mississippi River in Tennessee, some forty miles north of Memphis. Fort Pillow was an earthen fortification built by the Confederates. It later fell into Union hands, and the Federals built a redoubt inside the fortification. This was hardly an important installation, holding only about 300 Tennessee Unionists and 260 black troops. The existence of the Unionists and the black soldiers proved to be an irritant that the Confederates could not abide, however. On April 12, 1864, twenty-five hundred to three thousand Confederate cavalrymen under the command of former slaveholder, slave trader, and postwar head of the Ku Klux Klan Nathan Bedford Forrest attacked this fort.

The Confederates quickly drove the outmanned Federals out of the embankments and toward the river. Forrest demanded surrender, but at first the Federals refused. Then the fighting became more severe, and the black and white Unionists began throwing down their arms. The Confederates continued shooting and killing anyway. By the next morning, only about sixty-five of the black soldiers had survived the slaughter. It was a massacre of the worst sort, although Forrest and his defenders long insisted that he bore no blame. Even in modern times, despite evidence to the contrary, apologists absolve Forrest of any responsibility for the horrible killing.[16]

News of the bloodbath reached Washington. Abraham Lincoln was scheduled to speak at a sanitary fair for Union soldiers in Baltimore, once the scene of an anti-Union riot in 1861. It was at this philanthropic bazaar to raise funds for medical and humanitarian aid for Federal soldiers that Lincoln talked about the horror at Fort Pillow. At the beginning of the war, he pointed out, there had been little thought of black men becoming soldiers, but now it was being done as a matter of course. Lincoln said he took full responsibility: "I am responsible for it to the American people, to the Christian world, to history, and on my final account to God. Having determined to use the negro as a soldier, there is no way but to give him all the protection given to any other soldier." At this point, Lincoln said, he did not know exactly what had happened at Fort Pillow, but once that had been definitively determined, "it will be matter of grave consideration in what exact course to apply the retribution; but in the supposed case, it must come."[17]

Lincoln asked his cabinet to study the incident. He believed that a massacre had taken place, but, he said, "the evidence is not yet quite ready to be laid before me." All the cabinet members agreed that the Confederates should be allowed to tell their side of the story, and then a decision as to how to respond should be made. Two weeks later, Lincoln told Stanton to let the Confederates know "that the government of the United States has satisfactory proof of the massacre by insurgent forces at Fort Pillow." He said further in this letter, which apparently was never sent, that the national government would not retaliate if it received assurances that such a massacre would never happen again. Additionally, if Confederates proved willing to exchange black soldiers for equal numbers of their own, all would be well, but if they refused, "it will be assumed by the government of the United States, that said captured colored troops shall have been murdered, or subjected to Slavery, and that said government will, upon said assumption, take such action as may then appear expedient and just."[18]

Lincoln came face-to-face with the results of the slaughter when the wife of Major Lionel F. Booth, the white commander killed at the fort, visited the president and made a point that he said was "very worthy of consideration." She suggested that "widows and children . . . of colored soldiers who fall in our service, be placed in law, the same as if their marriages were legal, so that they can have the benefit of provisions made [to] the widows & orphans of white soldiers," Lincoln told Radical Republican senator Charles Sumner. It was this letter that apparently prompted Congress to provide equal treatment for widows and orphans of the black troops.[19]

As Lincoln was trying to deal with this terrible event, Grant was in the process of organizing the Union army for its spring offensive. Consequently, the nation's attention shifted from Fort Pillow. Grant and his friend Sherman, commander of the Military Division of the Mississippi, traveled to Louisville and Cincinnati to plan their coordinated attacks on the Confederate army. The plan was for Grant to travel with the Army of the Potomac, led by George G. Meade, while Sherman was to go after Joseph E. Johnston in Georgia. The war was entering yet another new phase. Union armies would no longer simply mass against geographic locations; rather, they would battle Confederate armies all over the nation at the same time. Lincoln had been calling for just this sort of warfare for a long time, and finally he had a commanding general who agreed with him and was ready to act accordingly.

Grant simultaneously demonstrated his confidence in Sherman. In April 1864, he ordered Sherman to view Johnston's Confederates as his focus but left the details of the campaign to him. Sherman promised to keep pressure on Johnston, but if the opportunity arose, he would capture Atlanta too.[20]

Wanting to make sure Grant understood that he supported him, Lincoln wrote him a letter of encouragement. "I wish to express . . . my entire satisfaction with what you have done," he said. "The particulars of your plans I neither know, or seek to know. You are vigilant and self-reliant; and, pleased with this, I wish not to obtrude any constraints or restraints upon you." Lincoln promised to help in any way he could, however, and ended by stating, "And now with a brave Army, and a just cause, may God sustain you."[21]

Grant's response could not have been more pleasing to Lincoln. It showed how different he was from all the earlier generals Lincoln had dealt with in the Virginia theater. Grant "acknowledged with pride" all Lincoln's good words. During this war, he said, "I have never had cause of complaint" about Lincoln or Stanton, "for throwing any embarrassment in the way of my vigorously prosecuting what appeared to me my duty." In fact, he said, he was "astonished at the readiness" with which the Lincoln administration had provided everything he had requested. And in a sentence that must have particularly thrilled

Lincoln, Grant wrote, "Should my success be less than I desire, and expect, the least I can say is, the fault is not with you." Lincoln was clearly impressed with Grant and said, "He has the *grit* of a bulldog! Once let him get his 'teeth' *in*, and nothing can shake him off."[22]

Sherman was not as cooperative with Lincoln as was Grant. When Lincoln asked Sherman to modify an order the general had issued keeping reporters and civilians off the trains in his area, Sherman refused. He told Lincoln that experience had shown him "that the railroad cannot supply the army & the people too." Holding firm, he stated, "I will not change my order and I beg of you to be satisfied that the clamor is partly humbug." Lincoln backed off. He did not want to argue with his military. He wanted cooperation and steady forward progress.[23]

Grant and Sherman began their movements simultaneously in early May 1864—Grant against Lee in Virginia, and Sherman against Johnston in Georgia. At the same time, Grant called for Benjamin Butler to push up the James River from Fortress Monroe, while Franz Sigel moved up the Shenandoah Valley. When Lincoln heard of this strategy, he came up with one of his classic statements: "Those not skinning can hold a leg."[24]

Lincoln was clearly enthusiastic about Grant's forward determination. When a military band led a crowd to the Executive Mansion and serenaded the president, Lincoln expressed his satisfaction at Grant's early battlefield successes. He urged everyone to "follow the example of the modest general at the head of our armies, and sink all personal considerations for the sake of country." A Pennsylvania woman was worried about Lincoln's health under all the stress he was experiencing, and he thanked her for her concern and admitted, "I have been very anxious for some days in regard to our armies in the field, but am considerably cheered, just now, by favorable news from them."[25]

But not all the news was so positive. On May 17, 1864, the *New York World* and *New York Journal of Commerce* published a bogus proclamation, allegedly coming from Lincoln and the secretary of state, calling for "a day of fasting, humiliation and prayer" and a new draft of four hundred thousand men because of "military problems all over the nation." Lincoln was furious and railed against this "false and spurious proclamation . . . of a treasonable nature, designed to give aid and comfort to the enemies of the United States, and to the rebels now at war against the Government, and their aiders and abettors." He ordered the immediate arrest and imprisonment of the officials of these papers and anyone else involved.

Publishers and editors of other newspapers quickly responded, blaming the proclamation on a quirk in the Associated Press system that could fool any newspaper at any time. They asked Lincoln to rescind the arrest order, because "the suspension" of two newspapers "has had the effect to awaken editors & publishers and news agents, telegraph companies etc. to the propriety of increased vigilance in their several duties." Lincoln was convinced. After two days, he had Stanton lift the suspension, allowing the newspapers back on the street and releasing their editors from jail. Joseph Howard, the reporter who caused the bogus proclamation to be published in the first place, remained incarcerated until August 23.[26]

The 1864 presidential election was never far from Lincoln's mind during this period. The intrigues of Salmon P. Chase and other Republicans notwithstanding, Lincoln easily received the nomination of the National Union Party, as the Republicans now labeled themselves. The party platform followed Lincoln's wishes. He insisted on the inclusion of a provision calling for the passage of a Thirteenth Amendment to the Constitution to eliminate slavery throughout the United States. He worried that because he had issued the Emancipation Proclamation based on his wartime powers, slave freedom might be lost once the war was over. He also worried that the Supreme Court, under Roger B. Taney's leadership, might declare emancipation to be a violation of the Fifth Amendment.

The National Union Party convention endorsed the Emancipation Proclamation and the use of black soldiers, insisting "that the Government owes to all men employed in its armies, without regard to distinction of color, the full protection of the laws of war." Any violation of this principle on the part of the enemy "should be made the subject of prompt and full redress." The call for a Thirteenth Amendment was even more unequivocal: "Resolved, That as Slavery was the cause and constitutes the strength of this Rebellion, and as it must be, always and everywhere, hostile to the principles of Republican Government, justice and National safety demand its utter and complete extirpation from the soil of the Republic."[27]

This was an amazing statement. In 1861, another Thirteenth Amendment had been offered in Congress, that one *guaranteeing* slavery in the states. Now, just three years later, the National Union Convention proposed a Thirteenth Amendment that called for the elimination of slavery throughout the nation. Lincoln's steady argument was convincing the nation that the war for the Union could be won only if slavery was eliminated. Congress still had to accept this amendment and pass it along to the states for ratification, but the enthusiasm for it at Lincoln's convention augured well for its future passage. Yet there was no guarantee that this amendment would become part of the Constitution. Did white people in the North have the patience and perseverance to continue fighting for black freedom as Lincoln insisted? Many Northerners held racist attitudes. Lincoln received information that in Kentucky, for example, "our military are seizing negroes and carrying them off without their own consent, and according to no rules whatever, except those of absolute violence." Lincoln wanted such activity to stop, but the fact that it was even happening at this time in the war was disconcerting.[28]

There was also the major question as to whether black soldiers should receive the same pay as white soldiers. On June 15, 1864, Congress voted to provide equal pay for all black soldiers, but it made the pay rate retroactive to the date of enlistment only for those who had been free on April 19, 1861. The unfairness was obvious to Lincoln, but he decided not to act on it himself because he worried that it would create problems with the white Union soldiers. Instead, he asked for and received a legal opinion from his attorney general, Edward Bates, a conservative Republican from the Union slave state of Missouri, who provided an answer "unhesitatingly" that all black soldiers, no matter the time of their freedom, should be paid the same as whites. Edwin M. Stanton endorsed this letter and sent it to the army paymaster general with orders that black soldiers should forthwith be paid in accordance with Bates's legal opinion.[29] It took until March 1865 for the Federal government to implement the policy of full back pay for all black soldiers to the time of their enlistment. Another important milestone in the war effort and in African American freedom had been achieved, and Lincoln had finessed it through.

Meanwhile, Grant was changing the mindset of the Army of the Potomac. In the past, when this army had met Lee and his Confederates, it was all too ready to retreat. Now, no matter how the fighting went, Grant pressed forward. During the opening of the Overland Campaign, the fight in the Wilderness was bloody, but instead of falling back as the Army of the Potomac had done under previous generals, Grant stayed the course. Later, when he took a severe beating at Cold Harbor, he immediately began planning his next move. He decided to cross the James River toward Petersburg and secure that city, a gateway to Richmond. Lincoln's response to Grant's activity was brief yet encouraging: "I begin to see it. You will succeed. God bless you all." Grant was "the first General I have had," Lincoln told one of his secretaries. All the previous ones wanted to "put the responsibility of success or failure on me. They all wanted me to be the general. It wasn't so with Grant."[30]

At a sanitary fair in Philadelphia, Lincoln repeated his optimistic strain about the Federal military effort. "War, at the best, is terrible, and this war of ours . . . is one of the most terrible." It has hurt the nation in a variety of ways, and "it has carried mourning to almost every home, until it can almost be said that the 'heavens are hung in black,' Lincoln told his audience. "*We accepted this war; we did not begin it.*" He never liked to make predictions, Lincoln said, but he believed that Grant, with the aid of "the brave officers and soldiers with him," was "in a position from whence he will never be dislodged until Richmond is taken."

And then Lincoln brought the crowd to a high pitch. "If I shall discover that General Grant and the noble officers and men under him can be greatly facilitated in their work by a sudden pouring forward of men and assistance, will you give them to me? [Cries of 'yes.'] Then, I say, stand ready, for I am watching for the chance. [Laughter and cheers.]"[31]

Later that month, Lincoln, accompanied by his son Tad, visited Grant and his army in Virginia to get a closer look at the war there. It was a good visit, and Lincoln returned, as his secretary noted, "sun-burnt and fagged but still refreshed and cheered." He was pleased to see Grant and his men expressing confidence in the military future. As Lincoln was departing Grant's headquarters, the general even told him, "You Mr President, need be under no apprehension. You will never hear of me farther from Richmond than now, till I have taken it."[32] What a difference from his earlier generals, Lincoln must have thought yet again.

Lincoln also liked Grant's response to his inquiry about what to do with General Rosecrans. Grant had fired Rosecrans from his post as commander of the Army of the Cumberland, and he was now commanding troops in Missouri. Grant replied firmly, "The most useful way to employ Rosecrans would be to station him at some convenient point on the northern frontier with the duty of detecting & exposing rebel conspiracies in Canada."[33] Grant continued to have disdain for Rosecrans, but that general drove Sterling Price's forces out of Missouri in the early fall of 1864. After that, however, he played no major role in the rest of the war.

Despite Lincoln's renomination for the presidency, he still had to face a split Republican Party. The so-called Radical Republicans believed that he was moving too slowly on emancipation, while the conservatives thought he moved too quickly. Those in the middle lurched from side to side, sometimes supporting Lincoln, other times not. The Radical-dominated Joint Committee on the Conduct of the War tried to manage the conflict's direction and decide on its leaders. Lincoln worked to keep the committee at bay, but it was always a political problem for him. Some Radical Republicans even supported John C. Fremont on a splinter ticket, and Fremont only backed down when Lincoln removed the conservative Montgomery Blair from his cabinet.

As the presidential election heated up, Lincoln simultaneously had to deal with a Confederate attack on the nation's capital. Robert E. Lee sent Jubal Early's corps to rid the Shenandoah Valley of Union troops and to threaten Washington because Grant was putting pressure on Lee in Virginia. Most of the defenders of the capital city had earlier been sent to Grant, and the only soldiers left behind were invalids and weak militia. Trains stopped running, and the telegraph stopped clicking. Refugees from the countryside rushed into the city. Grant and Halleck were in regular correspondence, and on July 10, Lincoln reached out to Grant. He wanted his commanding general to hold on where he was but told him, "Bring the rest with you personally, and make a vigorous effort to destroy the enemie's [*sic*] force in this vicinity." As always, however, he added, "This is what I think, upon your suggestion, and is not an order."[34]

Fortunately for the Union cause, General Lew Wallace delayed Early at Monocacy, Maryland, on July 9, 1864, long enough that when Early arrived in front of Washington's Fort Stevens, Union troops, augmented with reinforcements from Grant's army, were ready. There was some minor skirmishing, but Early had to withdraw back to the Shenandoah Valley without doing any serious damage to the Union forces or the capital. Lincoln was present during the Fort Stevens action, his tall frame standing out in the entrenchments. He put himself in danger when his curiosity got the better of him. A captain who would later become a Supreme Court justice, Oliver Wendell Holmes Jr., allegedly yelled at him to get down. Lincoln obeyed.[35]

Lincoln's problems persisted. Some of them were exasperating continuations of those he had endured throughout the war, but others provided hope for the future. He continued to struggle with his generals, finding most of them unwilling or unable to provide the kind of leadership the war effort needed, and he had to initiate another draft to fill manpower needs in the army. The press remained a problem. Bloody fighting rather than clear progress on the battlefield seemed the order of the day. Race relations appeared to be better than ever with the Republican call for a Thirteenth Amendment plus the ruling on equal pay, yet the Confederates had massacred black soldiers at Fort Pillow, and whites had massacred black residents in racist draft riots in New York City on July 13–16, 1863.[36] Kentucky, which previously had tried to be neutral, now was upset when it learned that Union troops would be leaving its borders. However, a new general, Ulysses S. Grant, and a new leadership team were gaining more success on the battlefield and thus putting fewer demands on Lincoln to carry the full military load. Grant was driving Lee in Virginia, while Sherman was pushing Johnston in Georgia. Halleck loved his new position as chief of staff and was doing good logistical and administrative work.

Yet significant problems remained. A Confederate raid on Washington had proven disturbing. In fact, disappointment hovered over every battlefield. Injury and death were the order of the day, and war-weariness seemed to be growing. Confederates were determined to hold on, while the future of black people in the nation as well as that of the seceded states hung in the balance.

Lincoln's reelection thus was crucial for a successful completion of the war. But there was no guarantee that he would be reelected. Lincoln worried that Democratic nominee George B. McClellan might very well win. If he did, would this mean an end to the war and a return to the old Union of slavery? No one knew for sure, but most people, North and South, believed that the outcome of the war would be determined in the results of the November 1864 presidential polls.

CHAPTER EIGHT

"A VICTORY WORTH MORE . . . THAN A BATTLE WON"

During the summer of 1864, Lincoln had to face the reality that the North was suffering war-weariness, and the Confederates were more than willing to take advantage of such feelings. In July of that year, Horace Greeley of the *New York Tribune* received a proposal from officials of the Confederate government for peace negotiations. He consulted with Lincoln, who realized what the Confederates had in mind. Yet Lincoln decided to let the negotiations go on and asked Greeley to be one of the negotiators. The New York editor was not pleased with that development, but he acquiesced. He arrived at the site of the talks, Niagara Falls, Ontario, on July 17.

Greeley carried instructions from the president, who had written a "To Whom It May Concern" letter in which he said that his administration would consider any proposal that included "the restoration of peace, the integrity of the whole Union, and the abandonment of slavery." The Confederate commissioners denied having any power to negotiate peace, although they admitted that they were in the secret employ of the Confederate government—that is, they were spies. They refused Lincoln's terms, so the talks broke up.[1] Lincoln had won an important victory. He had shown his willingness to talk peace, yet he plainly would do so only on the basis of Union and the end of slavery, something he knew the Confederacy would not accept. Greeley's enthusiasm was quenched, and the military effort was not harmed.

Lincoln saw more than negotiations involved in the visit of the Confederate commissioners. As they had no power to agree to a peace settlement, Lincoln was convinced that they had come from the South for ulterior reasons: "Does any one doubt that what they *are* empowered to do, is to assist in selecting and arranging a candidate and a platform for the Chicago [Democratic] convention?" The only terms they would suggest would be "independence of the South—the dissolution of the Union."[2] Lincoln said he would never accept such terms.

When word got out about this meeting, Charles D. Robinson, a newspaper editor from Green Bay, Wisconsin, and a War Democrat, was critical of Lincoln's actions. He said that the meeting with Confederate commissioners was a complete change from the letter Lincoln had written to Greeley in 1862, when he had said that he would save the Union, if it came to that, without freeing one slave. But he had freed slaves and incorporated black soldiers into the military, the War Democrat said, and he was disgruntled. Lincoln responded in mid-August 1864, saying that his Greeley letter had asserted that he would free the slaves if that was necessary to win the war. He had believed that it was necessary, so he had done it. He had no plan to change that position.[3]

Lincoln also demonstrated that he was going to stay involved in the war planning. He met with Grant at a summer 1864 Fortress Monroe meeting. No records have survived, but the two men likely had a frank discussion in which Lincoln displayed his unhappiness with all that had transpired recently, especially the heavy casualties in Virginia. Later Grant wrote the president that he wanted General Phil Sheridan to have command of the Union army in the Shenandoah Valley and then wanted him to "put himself South of the enemy, and follow him to the death. Wherever the enemy goes, let our troops go also." Lincoln responded to Grant that this would not be done "unless you watch it every day, and hour, and force it." Grant immediately went to Washington and then to the Federal army in the valley. He forced it, and Sheridan replaced David Hunter and went on the offensive. Again, it was Lincoln who made a suggestion, but this time he had a general in place who immediately accomplished it.[4]

Notwithstanding the meeting, the battles in Virginia remained bloody, and the public desire to end the carnage grew. Grant remained steadfast that he would not withdraw, and Lincoln supported him completely. "I have seen your dispatch expressing your unwillingness to break your hold where you are," he said. "Neither am I willing. Hold on with a bull-dog grip, and chew & choke as much as possible."[5]

Grant held on, but there seemed no end to the fighting. The bloodletting was particularly worrisome for Lincoln's reelection. It was not considered proper for a presidential candidate, not even an incumbent president, to campaign, so there was little Lincoln could do on his own behalf. He needed a quick victory on the battlefield to destroy the war-weariness sweeping the North, and once again, Lincoln tried to make it happen.

Lincoln reached out to the common soldiers, as he had tried to do throughout the war. In mid-August, he told the commanding general of a militia unit from Ohio, about to return home, that he would be happy to have the regiment come to the Executive Mansion so he could speak to the men. He wanted to make sure that these soldiers understood that "in this great struggle, this form of Government and every form of human right is endangered if our enemies succeed." He also appealed for their votes when he said he knew that inequities existed in the federal government, such as in the taxing system, but there was just no time to correct everything before any tax was collected. He reminded the men, "This struggle is too large for you to be diverted from it by any small matter." Two weeks later, when addressing another Ohio unit, he emphasized the same war and election point. "The constitutional administration of our government must be sustained," he said, "and I beg of you not to allow your minds or your hearts to be diverted from the support of all necessary measures for that purpose, by any miserable picayune arguments addressed to your pockets, or inflammatory appeals made to your passions or your prejudices."[6]

When Lincoln met with the abolitionist ex-governor of Wisconsin Alexander W. Randall and journalist Joseph T. Mills, he once again emphasized the importance of the forthcoming election. He particularly insisted that it made absolutely no sense to insist on the return of African Americans, including black soldiers, to slavery. He found it upsetting that some people argued that he would carry on the war until all the slaves were free. Not so, he said. His goal had always been and continued to be "the sole purpose of restoring the Union." However, he stated, "No human being can subdue the rebellion without using the Emancipation lever as I have."[7]

No matter what he said, everyone continued predicting that he had no chance of reelection. The political wizard Thurlow Weed told Secretary of State William H. Seward that he had told Lincoln a week previously that "his re-election was an impossibility." "The People are wild for Peace," Weed wrote. "They are told that the president will only listen to terms of Peace on condition Slavery is 'abandoned.'" Henry J. Raymond, a journalist and Republican leader, believed that "commissioners should be immediately sent, to Richmond, offering to treat for Peace on the basis of Union."[8] Lincoln's juncture of freedom and union seemed on the verge of collapse.

Seemingly sure that his reelection chances were gone, Lincoln did something almost unimaginable. He wrote a memorandum that came to be called the "blind memo," in which he promised to "so co-operate with the President elect, as to save the Union between the election and the inauguration." He placed it in an envelope, and then had the members of his cabinet sign the envelope without knowing its contents.[9]

Yet Lincoln did not stop trying to find the road to victory. He wrote to Raymond that he should arrange, "if possible, a conference for peace with Hon. Jefferson Davis," and instructed him, "At said conference you will propose, on behalf of this government, that upon the restoration of the Union and the national authority, the war shall cease at once, all remaining questions [such as emancipation] to be left for adjustment by peaceful modes. If this be accepted hostilities to cease at once." If these terms were not acceptable to Davis, Lincoln told Raymond to ask what terms would be. Before he sent this letter, however, Lincoln met in conference with Raymond, Secretary of State Seward, Secretary of War Stanton, and Republican senator William P. Fessenden. The meeting resulted in the letter being shelved, as the participants believed that even worse than losing the election was surrendering before the election even took place.[10]

This decision could not have come at a better time. Word arrived in Washington that William T. Sherman had captured Atlanta and Admiral David G. Farragut had won a naval victory in Mobile Bay and sealed off the city of Mobile. On September 3, 1864, Lincoln happily ordered a hundred-gun salute in Union cities all across the nation. He also called on people in the North to offer prayers and thanksgiving for all the signal victories.[11] It was as though the clouds had lifted and the sun was shining on the Federal cause—and on Lincoln's reelection hopes.

At about the same time, a bizarre problem reared its head. On September 10, the *New York World* published an alleged account of Lincoln's visit to Antietam shortly after the end of the battle in 1862. According to the newspaper, Lincoln, McClellan, an unnamed officer, and longtime Lincoln friend and District of Columbia marshal Ward Lamon were riding in an ambulance, viewing the horrible sights. As the ambulance reached Burnside's Bridge, a site of terrible slaughter, Lincoln purportedly turned to Lamon and said, "Come, Lamon, give us that song about Picayune Butler; McClellan has never heard it." McClellan supposedly protested such a lack of respect for the dead, but the song went on.

After the publication of the accusatory article, an individual wrote to Lamon and wanted to know if this event had actually happened. Lamon passed this letter on to the president, who wrote a detailed account of his four-day visit to McClellan in which he indicated that Lamon had sung a sad song on Lincoln's request, and then someone else had asked for something lighter, which Lamon provided. "Neither Gen. McClellan or any one else made any objection to the singing; the place was not on the battle field, the time was sixteen days after the battle, no dead body was seen during the whole time the president was absent from Washington, nor even a grave that had not been rained on since it was made." Fortunately for Lincoln, the story apparently died off on its own.[12]

Word also got to Lincoln that army officers were increasingly upset over his administration's interpretation of War Department Circular

No. 61, which called for anyone serving his three years of service to count months not from the time he first entered the military, but from his "last promotion and remuster." This meant that some soldiers could end up serving five years to meet their three-year obligation. Lincoln asked Grant what he thought, and Grant told him the circular was indeed creating hard feelings, saying, "many valuable officers are refusing promotion." Grant asked that all individuals should serve three years and no more. Lincoln accepted these changes and avoided a major military and reelection problem. When Lincoln then came under attack for allegedly interfering with Grant and other generals, Grant said he believed Lincoln should just ignore such charges. "To attempt to answer all the charges the opposition will bring against him will be like setting a maiden to work to prove her chastity."[13]

The issue of peace negotiations and the reason for the Union war effort remained major problems, however. Lincoln was invited to a Union mass meeting in Buffalo where he would have to confront the emancipation issue again. He did not go, but he sent a letter that stated his oft-repeated words that the reason for the war was indeed preservation of the Union, but without emancipation, the Union would be lost. "We cannot spare the hundred and forty or fifty thousand [black troops] now serving us as soldiers, seamen, and laborers. . . . Nor is it possible for any Administration to retain the service of these people with the express or implied understanding that upon the first convenient occasion, they are to be re-inslaved [*sic*]. It *can* not be; and it *ought* not to be," Lincoln insisted.[14]

As he struggled with these issues, Lincoln realized even more that he needed the soldier vote for victory. He thus encouraged his military leaders to do all they could to allow soldiers to cast their ballots. Most states allowed the soldiers to vote in the field, but Indiana was an October voting state, and it was also a state that did not allow its soldiers such absentee voting. Lincoln told William T. Sherman, always the most difficult to persuade, "Any thing you can safely do to let her soldiers, or any part of them, go home and vote at the State election, will be greatly in point." He even insisted that "they need not remain for the Presidential election." He did not want Sherman to think that this was "an order" and told him he should do whatever he could "safely do."[15] Sherman understood, and this time he cooperated. He allowed the soldiers to rush home to vote and rush back again to continue the war.

Even as he worried about the election, Lincoln continued to worry about the war. He obsessed about Lee trying to strengthen Jubal Early in the Shenandoah Valley in order for Early to attack Sheridan. Grant told the president not to worry because he would maintain his attacks on Lee and prevent him from sending any troops to the valley. Grant was now within six miles of Richmond, he reported. When Lincoln showed this letter to Stanton and Halleck, they shared his excitement. Stanton enthusiastically said that Grant "will be in Richmond tonight." Lincoln was not that enthusiastic and responded no before asking Halleck what he thought. Halleck said he believed that Grant would be in Petersburg or Richmond soon.[16]

Now that Lincoln could feel more confident about Virginia, he began worrying about Sherman's future plans. The redheaded general had captured Atlanta, and now he wanted to do something even more dramatic: turn Atlanta into a military post by sending civilians out of the city, cut himself from his supply line, and use psychological destructive warfare against Confederate society by marching through the heart of Georgia toward the sea. Sherman believed that if he could demonstrate that the Confederacy was a "hollow shell," the populace would recognize that its government and army could not protect it, and they would quit the conflict. Sherman did not want to continue fighting a war of death and maiming; rather, he wanted to break the Confederate will through property destruction. As for John Bell Hood's Confederate army, George H. Thomas would handle it.[17]

Grant and Lincoln were not sold on the idea. Both of them believed in the concept of destroying the opposition's army, so the thought of Hood at large in the countryside was frightening. They were convinced that Sherman should defeat Hood first before undertaking any march to the sea. Lincoln leaned heavily on Grant but wanted him to know that he worried about Sherman's plan, which he feared "might be fatal to his army." Grant agreed, but he also trusted Sherman implicitly. He accepted Sherman's plan, and Lincoln immediately followed along. He told the secretary of war that "Sherman's proposition is the best that can be adopted and Sherman & his army" would be "hard to corner or capture." Grant told Sherman, "If there is any way of getting at Hood's army, I would prefer that, but I must trust to your own judgment."[18]

In the East that summer, the Union war effort remained equally problematic. On July 30, 1864, an explosive was placed under the Confederate entrenchments in front of Ambrose Burnside's IX Corps, part of the siege line surrounding Petersburg, Virginia. An explosion created a giant hole in the line. Burnside had trained several regiments from a division of Colored Troops under the command of General Edward Ferrero to charge into the breach, but General Meade had decided that he did not want the black troops to conduct this operation because, if it failed, it would be said that the Federals were callously sacrificing black soldiers. Burnside protested, but Grant sided with Meade. No white division would volunteer, however, so Burnside chose one by lot to make the attack. Its commander provided no leadership; in fact, he was drunk during the operation. The untrained soldiers found themselves under unyielding fire and suffered huge losses in what was called the Battle of the Crater. Lincoln did not respond formally, no doubt discussing the events with Grant when they met at Fort Monroe the next day.[19]

A few months later in the Shenandoah Valley, in October 1864, Sheridan made his famous ride to rally Union troops to defeat Confederates at Cedar Creek and thus complete Union control of the valley. Lincoln did write to Sheridan, however, expressing "the thanks of the Nation, and my own personal admiration and gratitude."[20]

Throughout the war, Lincoln and his secretary of state, William H. Seward, had another worry: the possible intervention of the European nations. Lincoln was "horrified" at the idea of a war with England, while the French support for Maximilian against Juarez in Mexico was frightening because it would mean a European nation on the U.S.-Confederate borders and might result in French intervention in the war. The 1861 *Trent* Affair, when the U.S. Navy stopped a British mail packet carrying Confederate diplomats, might have led to conflict with Great Britain, but the Lincoln administration had kept the crisis from escalating. Lincoln's Emancipation Proclamation also dampened British interest in intervention. The Union blockade of Southern ports remained an irritant to Great Britain, however, and the British building of ships for the Confederacy similarly was upsetting to the Union. Fortunately for Lincoln, peace with Europe held, and after the war, diplomacy solved the lingering disagreements.

Yet as early as April 1864, concern about foreign intervention was never far from Lincoln's mind, as the Confederates tried to foment problems with other nations. On October 19, 1864, the Confederates made a bizarre invasion of St. Albans, Vermont, where they robbed banks, stole horses, and tried to burn down the city. Irate Vermonters chased the raiders toward the Canadian border, and most were caught, some inside Canada. Since Canada belonged to Great Britain, the raid created anti-British feeling and led to intensive diplomacy. Grant wanted to allow his military to chase the marauders into Canada, but Lincoln immediately refused to accept this idea for fear it would lead to British intervention. Grant was not happy, but as always, he acceded to Lincoln's wishes, and the incident quickly lost its diplomatic importance.[21]

The presidential election took place soon thereafter, on November 8. Lincoln was pleased that the nation supported his war efforts by reelecting him by over four hundred thousand votes. He was particularly happy that the soldiers voted for him overwhelmingly, particularly those in McClellan's old Army of the Potomac, which helped him carry New York and Connecticut. Grant's congratulations were also meaningful, particularly the sentence that read, "The election having passed off quietly, no bloodshed or rioit [*sic*] throughout the land, is a victory worth more to the country than a battle won."[22]

As Lincoln enjoyed the afterglow of the presidential election, William Tecumseh Sherman began the march through Georgia that Grant and Lincoln had at first opposed. They had believed that the Union armies had to destroy the Confederate armies, while Sherman believed that psychological destructive war was the road to victory. As Grant hammered away at Robert E. Lee's army in Virginia, Sherman left George H. Thomas to handle John Bell Hood and struck out against Confederate society in Georgia. Very few people were hurt or killed during Sherman's march, but there was much destruction.

Confederates grew upset and dismayed, and numbers of Lee's soldiers in Virginia deserted to go protect their homes and families. It seemed that there was no stopping Sherman. Lincoln remained concerned, however, as the general could potentially run out of supplies or be cut off, as Napoleon had been at Moscow in the early nineteenth century. And if Thomas did not handle Hood, an invasion of the North was also a possibility.

Sherman hid himself completely from the outside world. He cut the telegraph wires behind him as he left Atlanta, and the only news of his whereabouts during the march came from Southern newspapers that kept insisting that the Confederates had the Union general just where they wanted him. Federals did not know what to believe, and neither did Lincoln. During the march, the general's brother, John Sherman, asked if the president could inform him of his brother's whereabouts. Lincoln told him he knew nothing. "We know what hole he went in," he said, "but we don't know what hole he will come out of."

Sherman finally reappeared in mid-December near Savannah and wrote Lincoln a quick report that captivated the president and the nation. Since he had reached the Atlantic coast during the holiday season, he offered the captured city of Savannah to Lincoln as a Christmas present. Thus he became known as the Union's Santa Claus.[23]

Meanwhile, Thomas was shadowing Hood as the Confederate moved through Tennessee. On November 30, 1864, one of Thomas's subordinates, John M. Schofield, won a resounding victory at Franklin, Tennessee, resulting in huge Confederate casualties, including the deaths of six generals. Schofield then joined the rest of Thomas's army in the Nashville area, where they began making plans for a major battle against Hood. Unfortunately, Thomas had a reputation to match his nickname, "Slow Trot." He did not move quickly. Halleck tried to push Thomas, and Grant grew so impatient that he threatened to fire him and replace him with Schofield. Then an ice storm hit the Nashville area, and Thomas had another excuse to stand down. A frustrated Grant prepared an order to replace him with Schofield, but when Halleck heard about the ice storm, he persuaded Grant to hold off. The ice melted away on December 15, and Thomas finally went on the offensive and sent Hood's army reeling.

Grant and Halleck urged him to press the attack and complete the destruction, but Thomas said he could not, and he did not. No matter, Hood's army no longer existed as a viable military unit.[24] And Sherman's earlier predictions had been fulfilled: he had marched through Georgia demoralizing the Confederates, while his subordinate George H. Thomas had destroyed Hood's Army of Tennessee.

Throughout this fighting, Lincoln received only bits and pieces of news. In early December, Lincoln had joked with a crowd, "I have no good news to tell you, and yet I have no bad news to tell" either. He paraphrased the words he had said earlier to John Sherman about his brother's march to the sea: "We all know where he went in at, but I can't tell where he will come out at." After the first day at the battle of Nashville, Lincoln sent Thomas a note of encouragement and exhortation: "Please accept . . . the nation's thanks for your good work of yesterday. You made a magnificent beginning. A grand consummation is within your easy reach. Do not let it slip."[25]

Lincoln's most excited response to the military events of this period was his letter of thanks to Sherman: "Many, many, thanks for your Christmas-gift—the capture of Savannah," he wrote. Then he composed some heartfelt words of humility. He admitted that he had been "*anxious*, if not fearful," when Sherman had left Atlanta on his march, but he "did not interfere" because he believed his general "the better judge." As a result, he told Sherman, "the honor is all yours." Still, Lincoln could not contain his desire to end the war quickly. "But what next?" he inquired, seemingly impatient. "I suppose it will be safer if I leave Gen. Grant and yourself to decide." Lincoln was taking no chances. He liked what he was seeing from his generals, but he was not content to let them rest on their laurels.[26]

Earlier that month, he had struck a positive pose in his annual message to Congress on December 6, 1864. The overall impression he gave, however, was that the war was hardly over. Lincoln pointed out that the Union had not lost ground during 1864, and in Arkansas and Louisiana, some loyal individuals had organized state governments. Maryland, he was pleased to report, was "secure to Liberty and Union for all the future." He was also happy to announce that the Thirteenth Amendment, abolishing slavery in the United States, had passed the Senate. It had failed in the House of Representatives, but Lincoln was sure it was only a matter of time before it passed there too. The recent election indicated, he said, that "the purpose of the people, within the loyal States, to maintain the integrity of the Union, was never more firm, nor more nearly unanimous, than now."

Lincoln expressed certitude that the Confederacy was at the point of exhaustion. Its armies were running out of replacements for its depleted ranks. As for the North, he pointed out "that we have *more* men *now* than we had when the war *began*; that we are not exhausted, nor in process of exhaustion; that we are *gaining* strength, and may, if need be, maintain the contest indefinitely. . . . Material resources are now more complete and abundant than ever." Consequently, he said, any talk of negotiations was nonsensical. Confederates "can, at any moment, have peace simply by laying down their arms and submitting to the national authority under the Constitution. . . . If questions should remain, we would adjust them by the peaceful means of legislation, conference, courts, and votes, operating only in constitutional and lawful channels."

Lincoln also wanted it understood that, although this war was being fought to preserve the Union, he "retract[ed] nothing heretofore said as to slavery." He would not take back or change the Emancipation Proclamation. He insisted that he would not "return to slavery any person who is free by the terms of that proclamation, or by any of the Acts of Congress. If the people should, by whatever mode or means, make it an Executive duty to re-enslave such persons, another, and not I, must be their instrument to perform it."[27] Liberty and union remained Lincoln's goals. His recent reelection made his words that much more powerful. But nothing was guaranteed.

CHAPTER NINE

"HE WILL STAND IN HISTORY BESIDE WASHINGTON, PERHAPS HIGHER"

As 1864 drew to a close and the horrendous war was about to enter yet another year, Ulysses S. Grant felt confident about his ability to defeat Robert E. Lee, and William Tecumseh Sherman was preparing to take his destructive war from Georgia into the Carolinas. There was fighting yet to be done, and Lincoln remained eager to support his successful generals.

Upon Sherman's arrival on the Atlantic coast after his march through Georgia, an order from Grant awaited, calling on him to forget about taking Savannah. Instead, Grant told him to fortify his hold where he was, leave a force to secure it, and board his army on ships to carry them to Virginia to help close out Lee. Sherman was shocked. He had made his march to get away from the conventional warfare of killing that he so abhorred, yet Grant now wanted him to become part of that process again in Virginia. He protested, telling Grant that putting his men on cramped ships for passage to Virginia made less sense than marching them through the Carolinas and getting behind Lee that way. On December 27, 1864, Grant agreed. Sherman had his authority to march destructively through North and South Carolina. He would not have to return to the war of annihilation that he so detested.[1]

At the same time, Grant was terribly upset at the failure of General Benjamin F. Butler to take Wilmington, North Carolina. He wrote to Secretary of War Stanton that Butler had to go, pointing out that Butler, by right of rank, would take command any time Grant was absent. Unfortunately, Grant said, "there is a lack of confidence felt in his Military ability, making him an unsafe commander for a large Army." Besides, "his administration of his Department is also objectionable." Learning that Stanton was out of town, Grant wrote directly to Lincoln on January 6, 1865, asking for Butler's removal. The very next day, Halleck issued the directive. The day of the political general was passing. The war had reached the point where Lincoln needed competence more than he needed political influence.[2]

At this time, Lincoln believed that his military team knew what it was doing, so he did not correspond with them frequently. However, he was still very much involved in the conflict. In early January, Halleck received a letter from Sherman informing him of his plans for the march through the Carolinas, explaining that he would follow the same strategy that he had used in Georgia. Sherman said, "[I will] make a good ready and then move rapidly to my objective, avoiding a battle at points where I would be encumbered by wounded, but striking boldly and quickly when my objective is reached. I will give due heed and encouragement to all peace movements, but conduct war as though it could only terminate with the destruction of the enemy."[3]

Halleck shared this message with the president, and Lincoln liked very much of what he read. However, he did not see enough reference to quick movement. He liked the idea of Sherman's "*get a good ready*," he said, but "*time*, now that the enemy is wavering, is more important than ever before." Finding the enemy "on the down-hill, & somewhat confused," Sherman should be "keeping him going." Lincoln told Stanton to "say so much to Genl. S."[4] Lincoln still saw his role as encouraging his generals to keep pressure on the enemy.

At the same time, Lincoln had to face a personal matter. His son Robert had been at Harvard during most of the war but was becoming increasingly bothered that he had never served in the conflict. Complicating matters was Mary Lincoln's insistence that her son not join the army. She feared for his life, worried that she would lose him as she had earlier lost son Willie. Lincoln found himself caught between the wishes of his wife and his son, but he sided with Robert.

On January 19, he wrote to Grant "not [as] President, but only a friend," telling him that Robert, having recently graduated from Harvard, "wishes to see something of the war before it ends." He did not want him to see combat, Lincoln said, nor be given a rank that he did not deserve. Would Grant, "without embarrassment . . . or detriment to the service," take Robert into his "Military family with some nominal rank"? Lincoln said that he, not the public, would pay the costs. As he always told his generals, however, Lincoln said that Grant should not hesitate to say no.[5]

Grant replied quickly, "I will be most happy to have him in my Military family in the manner you propose." Robert then thanked Grant profusely, and on February 11, the young man was named a captain.[6] He did not serve very long or in any danger, but he was present at Lee's surrender at Appomattox. Grant once again had solved a problem for Lincoln, and the president was grateful.

At about the same time the young Lincoln was entering the army, Francis Preston Blair, an elderly Jacksonian and the father of Lincoln's postmaster general, decided to try to negotiate with his old friend Jefferson Davis to end the war and unite Grant's and Lee's armies against the French in Mexico. In the last days of December 1864, Lincoln had allowed Blair to make a trip to Richmond, where the elder statesman met with Davis on January 12, 1865. He pointed out to the Confederate president that he had no official position, but as a private citizen, he wanted to see what could be done to end the war. Davis gave him a letter to take to Washington expressing interest in a "conference with the view to secure peace to the two countries." Returning to Washington, Blair showed the letter to Lincoln, who immediately wrote back on January 18 that he had always been ready to talk about "securing peace to the people of our one common country."[7]

The divide between the two men was obvious. Davis talked about two countries, Lincoln about one. In Washington, the renewed movement to pass the Thirteenth Amendment and thus end slavery throughout the United States could also prove to be a major problem for the Confederacy. Blair passed Lincoln's letter on to Davis, and the Confederate leader appointed a commission consisting of Vice President Alexander H. Stephens, former Supreme Court Justice John

A. Campbell, and Confederate Senator R. M. T. Hunter to go north to pursue peace. Lincoln denied that any negotiations were planned for Washington, because many in the public feared that the passage of the Thirteenth Amendment would damage the chances for peace and thus the U.S. House of Representatives would balk at voting it in.[8]

The three Confederate commissioners reached Grant's headquarters at Hampton Roads and awaited news from Washington. On January 30, Lincoln sent Major Thomas T. Eckert to meet them. Seward, who followed shortly after Eckert, carried Lincoln's detailed requirements for any negotiations: "restoration of the national authority throughout all the States"; end of slavery as stated in Lincoln's annual message to Congress of 1864; "no cessation of hostilities short of an end of the war, and the disbanding of all forces hostile to the government."[9]

Despite the presence of these Confederate commissioners at Hampton Roads, Lincoln told Grant, "Let nothing which is transpiring, change, hinder, or delay your Military movements, or plans." He repeated that same thought on February 4. Grant understood. He told Lincoln, "The troops are kept in readiness to move at the shortest notice if occasion should justify it."[10]

Grant very much favored peace negotiations, so when Seward was recalled to Washington without having met with the Confederates, the general told Lincoln there would be major problems. Lincoln agreed. He wanted to make sure that there was no uncertainty as to where he stood: he would accept no peace except on the terms of one restored Union. Regarding freedom for the slaves, Lincoln said he himself would be willing to pay a tax to compensate Southerners for their financial losses, but he never brought up compensated emancipation. Yet the cabinet believed that Lincoln was willing to have the Federal government pay "the expenses of the war for two hundred days, or four hundred millions, to the Rebel States, to be [used] for the extinguishment of slavery, or for such purpose as the States were disposed." Gideon Welles, the secretary of the navy, believed such an idea had no chance of passage.[11]

Lincoln's meeting with the commissioners took place on February 3, 1865. He reported about it to the House of Representatives in a detailed February 10 memorandum filled with the complete text of the correspondence among all the principals. Lincoln reported that "the conference ended with no result." He had kept his cabinet in the dark, and to a man, "it struck them unfavorably that the Chief Magistrate should have gone on such a mission."[12]

The beginning of March 1865 saw yet another Confederate proposal for peace. Lee contacted Grant about holding an interview to devise a military convention to end the war. Through the secretary of war, Lincoln told Grant that under no circumstances should he talk peace with the Confederate general unless it involved the "capitulation" of Lee's army. Furthermore, he did not want Grant to discuss "any political question. Such questions the President holds in his own hands." As he had previously told Fremont and Hunter regarding antislavery pronouncements, Lincoln was determined to make such decisions himself.[13]

At the same time that such proposals were floating around, Lincoln continued to deal with a host of other war-related matters. Very troubling to Lincoln was the news that some of his army officers were still "forcing negroes into the Military service, and even torturing them." Lincoln wanted this stopped. It went against all he had been saying throughout the war. When Attorney General James Speed predicted that the Confederates would incorporate blacks into their army and even "give them commissions and make them officers," Lincoln disagreed. He said that "when they had reached that stage the cause of the war would cease and hostilities cease with it." Lincoln correctly realized that Confederate enlistment of African Americans would demonstrate that their cause was lost.[14]

Lincoln was uneasy about Sherman in the Carolinas and Sheridan in the Shenandoah Valley. He had consulted with Halleck, read a soothing message from Grant, and received a most favorable communication from Sheridan. All these activities "have relieved my anxiety," he told Grant. On March 2, Lincoln saw something ominous in the fact that the latest issues of the Richmond press had not reached him. Grant immediately reassured him that these had not been sent because there was nothing of interest in them. "There is every indication that Sherman is perfectly safe," Grant wrote on March 3. "I am looking every day for direct news from him." That same day, Lincoln demonstrated Grant's influence on him when he spoke briefly to a crowd of serenaders at the White House. "Sherman went in at Atlanta and came out right. He has gone in again at Savannah, and I propose three cheers for his coming out gloriously."[15]

There were more than three cheers the following day, when Lincoln was inaugurated for his second term on March 4, 1865. Despite the good feeling, the event was "confusion and without order—a jumble," particularly because of the "rambling and strange harangue" that Vice President Andrew Johnson made in his speech. Edwin M. Stanton said the new vice president was "either drunk or crazy." By contrast, Lincoln's speech was dignified and powerful. When he began speaking, the cloudy, rainy day turned sunny.

Lincoln's seven-hundred-word, four-paragraph speech is usually remembered for its last paragraph, beginning with the words "With malice toward none, with charity for all." In fact, though, there was a great deal more significance to this speech than its final words. Lincoln pointed out that four years previously, "both parties deprecated war; but one of them would *make* war rather than let the nation survive; and the other would *accept* war rather than let it perish. And the war came."

Continuing, Lincoln said that everyone realized that the existence of "colored slaves," primarily in the South, "was, somehow, the cause of the war. To strengthen, perpetuate, and extend this interest was the object for which the insurgents would rend the Union." No one could imagine in those early days "that the *cause* of the conflict might cease with, or even before, the conflict itself should cease." But in fact, the bloody war might go on "until all the wealth piled by the bond-man's two hundred and fifty years of unrequited toil shall be sunk, and until every drop of blood drawn with the lash, shall be paid by another drawn with the sword." It was God's will, and Lincoln seemed to believe that there was nothing he could do about it. Lincoln saw that all the bloodshed in the war was the result of divine justice, and he was God's mere instrument. As the abolitionist Frederick Douglass said in his diary, "The address sounded more like a sermon than a state paper." Lincoln saw that the speech did not receive a universally positive response and commented, "Men are not flattered by being shown that there has been a difference between the Almighty and them."[16]

As Lincoln began his second term, it was evident that the pressures of the war were draining him. Ever since his 1860 election, he had been engulfed in one controversy after another, and these were taking their toll. Although Grant and Sherman were now implementing the aggressiveness and achieving the victories that he had been hoping for throughout the war, the conflict was hardly over. Grant must have noticed the strain in his president, and in mid-March, he invited Lincoln to come to his headquarters at City Point, Virginia. "I would like very much to see you, and I think the rest would do you good," he said.[17]

Ever desirous to get close to the fighting, Lincoln answered immediately. He would come down the first chance he had, and he would bring Mrs. Lincoln with him. He arrived on the boat *River Queen*, bringing not only his wife but also his youngest child, Tad. For two weeks, he toured the Petersburg area and had frequent meetings with Grant and other military men. He enjoyed his time near the front and was pleased to learn more directly what Grant was doing. On March 29, for example, while Lincoln was at Grant's headquarters, the general sent him news about some military action and wrote as though Lincoln were familiar with the countryside where the skirmishing had taken place. When Lincoln told Stanton of his doings, the president seemed pleased to be able to report that he was "within five miles of the scene of . . . action."[18]

In fact, the war was drawing to a close. In the West, William T. Sherman had marched his army through the Carolinas and arrived in Goldsboro, North Carolina. He too decided to go to City Point to spend some time with Grant. He left on March 25 and arrived in Virginia by ship two days later. The two men greeted each other cordially, and soon Sherman was enthralling Grant and his subordinate officers with stories about his marches. After an hour, Grant told Sherman that Lincoln was on the *River Queen*, docked nearby, and they ought to go see him.

They walked over to the president's boat, and after mutual greetings, Lincoln sat listening in rapt interest to Sherman's stories. He repeatedly expressed concern about Sherman being away from his army. Did that not constitute danger? Sherman told the president that General John Schofield, whom he had left in charge, was more than capable of reacting to any threat.

The three men met again the following day, this time with U.S. Navy admiral David D. Porter also present. Lincoln told the military leaders that he was worried Robert E. Lee might try to break away from Grant and join Joe Johnston's Army of Tennessee to defeat Sherman. The redheaded general insisted that there was no danger of that happening. Besides, he could thwart both Confederate armies until Grant came to the rescue. Lincoln then worried about Johnston breaking away from Sherman and joining Lee, but Sherman insisted that would not happen either. He was convinced that within two weeks, he could force Johnston to accept any peace the Union wanted. Yet again, Lincoln expressed concern. In two weeks, Johnston might be able to turn the tide on Union forces. It would be better for Sherman to offer Johnston "the most liberal and honorable terms" and end the war immediately. "My God, my God, can't you spare more effusion of blood?" Lincoln begged. He also indicated that he would not mind it at all if Union forces allowed Confederate leaders to escape.[19]

There was no disagreement among the men at the meeting that the war was about to end. The generals went back to their armies, and Grant quickly was on the verge of driving Lee out of Richmond. Sherman continued his march through the Carolinas, expressing no concerns about Joe Johnston's skeleton force and coming up on Lee's rear. Lincoln had been disappointed so many times in the past that he still obsessed about the possibility of failure.

Lincoln remained with Grant's army in Virginia, so he continued to know more about what was happening there than he knew about Sherman's activities farther south. He told Stanton, "I begin to feel that I ought to be at home, and yet I dislike to leave without seeing nearer to the end of General Grant's present movement." Stanton realized Lincoln's excitement and told the president to stay where he was because his "presence will have great influence" on speeding Richmond's fall.[20]

The good news kept coming in. On April 2, 1865, the Federals broke through the entrenchments encircling Petersburg; they captured the city the next day and went after Lee's retreating army. Grant asked Lincoln to move closer to the fighting, and the president and son Tad did. In Washington, Stanton again worried about the president's safety. "Allow me respectfully to ask you to consider whether you ought to expose the nation to the consequence of any disaster to yourself in the pursuit of a treacherous and dangerous enemy like the rebel army." Lincoln appreciated Stanton's concern, but he told him that he had already been in Petersburg, and as Richmond had just been captured, he planned to visit it the next day. "I will take care of myself," he promised.[21]

Lincoln hurried forward to see for himself what he had been working for the past four years. Grant had achieved what Lincoln had been calling for all this time: the destruction of the Confederate army and, following on this, the capture of Richmond. "On to Richmond" had been one of the earliest demands of the nation. Grant had now accomplished that, and there was no one happier than Lincoln. "Allow me to tender to you, and all with you, the nations [*sic*] grateful thanks for this additional, and magnificent success," he said. Later, he wrote Grant one more word of advice. "Gen. Sheridan says: 'If the thing is pressed I think that Lee will surrender.' Let the *thing* be pressed."[22]

Lincoln could not wait to see for himself the city that had caused him so much heartache. On April 4, he left City Point and traveled with son Tad to see the Confederacy's capital. As soon as he arrived in the city, Richmond's slaves immediately recognized him. Admiral David D. Porter, who accompanied Lincoln, described the mobs of African Americans surrounding the president, some even kneeling before him. He was obviously embarrassed and said that they should kneel only to God. Lincoln wanted to get to the White House of the Confederacy, but the crowds of well-wishers slowed his progress to a crawl. The Union military finally was able to extricate Lincoln and get him to Jefferson Davis's former headquarters, where he wanted to speak to the officer in charge of the city. Instead, he found Virginians wishing to talk to him about peace. Grant was still pursuing

Lee's tattered army, and as there might still be hard fighting ahead, Lincoln did not say much.

Lincoln and Tad were then provided a carriage for a tour around the city. They spent the night aboard a Union naval vessel, and the next morning, Lincoln spoke to other white Virginians, the Confederates hoping for a quiet end to the conflict. Lincoln particularly conversed with former U.S. Supreme Court justice John A. Campbell, who had been one of the peace commissioners at Hampton Roads. Campbell's sincere desire for peace so impressed Lincoln that he gave him a paper listing the terms he had previously given Seward. These included restoration of the Union with slavery gone. Lincoln also promised that the nation would compensate slaveholders for their losses, if they acted immediately. Campbell thought that the sitting Virginia state legislature would accept these terms, and Lincoln told Major General Godfrey Weitzel, the military man in command of the area, to allow a meeting of these individuals. That same morning, the navy ship took Lincoln back to City Point, but Lee's surrender to Grant on April 9 at Appomattox Court House ended any need for peace talks.[23]

When news of Lee's surrender became known, Lincoln addressed an excited crowd at the Executive Mansion in Washington. He said that the taking of Petersburg and Richmond, along with "the surrender of the principal insurgent army, give hope of a righteous and speedy peace." He gave credit to God. Although he "was near the front" himself, he said, "no part of the honor, for plan or execution is mine. To Gen. Grant, his skillful officers and brave men, all belongs."

Grant's great success meant that there must now be "the re-inauguration of the national authority—reconstruction—which has had a large share of thought from the first," said Lincoln. "It is fraught with great difficulty," he explained, because "there is no authorized organ for us to treat with. No one man has authority to give up the rebellion for any other man." And "the loyal people" had no agreement as to how to accomplish it.

Lincoln knew that the end of the war did not necessarily mean the end of his problems. He was already being attacked for his role in trying to begin reconstruction of Louisiana. He had been open about his ideas, stating them forthrightly in his 1863 annual message. The Louisiana legislature had extended the Emancipation Proclamation to the entire state and had also ratified the Thirteenth Amendment, recently passed by Congress. The twelve thousand people in the state who supported the Union wanted to return to it as soon as they could, and they needed to be supported, Lincoln said. "Now, if we reject, and spurn them, we do our utmost to disorganize and disperse them. We in effect say to the white men 'you are worthless, or worse—we will neither help you, nor be helped by you.' To the blacks we say 'This cup of liberty which these, your old masters, hold to your lips, we will dash from you, and leave you to the chances of gathering the spilled and scattered contents in some vague and undefined when, where, and how.' . . . If, on the contrary, we recognize, and sustain the new government of Louisiana the converse of all this is true." And, Lincoln promised, if there was something he could do about the future for the South, he should "not fail to act."[24]

This was Lincoln's last speech. He never had the chance to speak publicly again. On the afternoon of April 14, 1865, he told his wife that both of them had to be "more cheerful in the future." That evening, he was shot while attending a play at Ford's Theatre. He died the next morning at 7:22. He had accomplished his military desire of saving the Union and ending slavery, but his future plans for a restored Union of liberty remained unaccomplished. George Templeton Strong, who had described Lincoln insultingly in the fall of 1861, now remarked, "No prince, no leader of a people, was ever so lamented as this unpolished Western lawyer has been and is. His name is Faithful and True. He will stand in history beside Washington, perhaps higher."[25]

CONCLUSION

Historians in the modern age agree that Abraham Lincoln ranks among the greatest of all American presidents. Surely much of that positive evaluation is the result of the leadership he demonstrated during the nation's greatest internal crisis, the Civil War. During the war, however, there was little agreement among contemporaries that he possessed greatness. Many, including Lincoln, even believed that he would not be reelected to the presidency in 1864. The nation seemed ready to end the war with the Old Union back as it had been in 1861, with slavery still part of the law of the land.

During the early part of Lincoln's first four years in office, he appeared to be an uneducated product of the midwestern frontier, thrashing about trying to find a solution to the multitude of problems he faced. He wanted to preserve the Union, and he realized that to do so, he had to lead the United States to victory in the horrendous Civil War. Over time, he came to see that to win, he had to attack that which had brought on the war in the first place: slavery. There was no doubt in his mind that he could constitutionally keep slavery out of the territories. However, the Constitution, which he revered and was determined to follow, protected the South's "peculiar institution" where it already existed. Although that document did provide a mechanism for change, an amendment to end slavery was hardly possible during the war. As a former member of the Whig Party and as an attorney, Lincoln worked from the premise that during wartime, the Constitution gave him the power to take actions that he could not take in time of peace. Thus he promulgated the Emancipation Proclamation to end slavery in areas still in rebellion against the United States. Having taken that initial step, he then pushed through the passage of the Thirteenth Amendment, which constitutionally eliminated slavery everywhere. Part of Lincoln's greatness lay in his ability to accomplish this revolutionary change in such a short time.

When war was thrust on him at Fort Sumter, he had to develop ideas, such as compensated emancipation, to keep the loyal border states in the Union fold and thus make it possible for the war effort to be successful. Should he lose the border states, especially Kentucky, he did not think the Union war effort would succeed. He could not, therefore, attack slavery directly. He knew that if he did, it would be for naught if it caused him to lose the war. He recognized early that destroying the South's institution of slavery was instrumental to victory, so he moved in that direction, but slowly and constitutionally.

Before the war, Lincoln had served in the militia, and this experience gave him a feeling for the Civil War's common soldiers, whom he visited many times during the war and whose affection he gained. He also displayed personal courage, demonstrated by his appearance near the front in battle. But his militia experience hardly gave him any knowledge of how to undertake the grand task of providing leadership to a nation at war. He had to learn quickly and well the complexities of strategy and tactics. This meant learning the conventional wisdom on these topics, contained in a variety of military tracts and in the minds of the military leaders of his time. Initially accepting his own military ignorance, he turned to generals like Winfield Scott and Henry W. Halleck to instruct him. He read all he could, and he listened as much as possible. He learned steadily, until he realized that he had actually begun to comprehend war better than his generals, and now he had to educate them.

One crucial job for Lincoln was to appoint generals in command of the armies who could win the war. This was a terribly difficult task, because successful generals require knowledge, ability, and the right temperament, qualities that are not always obvious to an observer. Consider how many military men Lincoln hired and fired while trying to find the individuals able to do the job the nation needed:

Winfield Scott, George B. McClellan, Ambrose Burnside, Joseph Hooker, George G. Meade, Don Carlos Buell, William Rosecrans, Benjamin Butler, Nathaniel Banks, and a host of others. These were not bad men; they simply lacked basic intangibles they needed for military success, including the ability to grow and develop.

Additionally, Lincoln sometimes had to appoint political generals to ensure the support of every element in American society, whether geographic or ethnic. Most of these generals did not have the qualities to be great leaders, although some, such as John A. Logan and Francis P. Blair, did. Lincoln also had to appoint some militarily incompetent individuals, because he needed their support and because the soldiers were attracted to them and enlisted as a result.

Lincoln not only had to choose military leaders but also had to make sure that they represented the length and breadth of the nation. Then he often had to cajole and threaten them, as well as educate them on how to fight a winning war. The old methodology of massing one's troops against fractions of the enemy simply did not work any longer. In this war, with the United States having the advantage in numbers, it was necessary to attack all along the line to prevent the Confederates from shifting troops in response to a possible massed Union attack in one particular place. Lincoln realized this fact early in the war; his generals did not. He saw the importance of attacking quickly and pushing forward, destroying the enemy's forces in the process. His early generals believed that careful preparation and the capture of places, not the destruction of armies, was war's necessity. He had to convince them otherwise.

What Lincoln wanted from his generals was their ability and willingness to provide leadership, and thus take some of the pressure off him. He had a tremendous amount of political and governmental work to do as a wartime president, so he needed help on the military side. He made a very important decision when he appointed Edwin M. Stanton as his secretary of war, and Stanton came through. So did Secretary of the Navy Gideon Welles, but the rest of his cabinet and Congress did not. They regularly placed more pressure on him than they helped alleviate. While Lincoln had to lead the war effort, he also had to consider a host of nonmilitary issues. These included important matters such as the construction of a transcontinental railroad, issuance of legal tender, creation of the Department of Agriculture, formation of the state of West Virginia, and passage of the Morrill Land-Grant Act, as well as more typical concerns such as patronage and government finances. Consequently, Lincoln could not spend all of his time focusing on the war, but he could not ignore it either, because the conflict controlled everything. He craved any help he might receive from the generals who were supposed to have the knowledge he purportedly did not have.

The decisive turning point in his war leadership came when, in 1864, he decided to make what proved to be his final change of generals. Lincoln made Ulysses S. Grant commanding general and appointed his predecessor, Henry W. Halleck, to a new office, chief of staff. In the West, he made William T. Sherman commander of that theater. He now had military leadership, Stanton included, that would take the weight off his shoulders. It was not the case, as some historians have insisted, that Lincoln took a hands-off attitude toward Grant and let him do what he wished. In truth, Lincoln and Grant agreed on the need to attack at every point simultaneously and to press forward. No matter the results of the previous engagement, the Union army should not falter or retreat. Grant took what Lincoln, Stanton, and Halleck provided for him, did not complain or make excuses, and fought. He kept the pressure on Robert E. Lee and his army in Virginia, while his close friend Sherman did the same against Joseph E. Johnston and John Bell Hood in Georgia, the Carolinas, and Tennessee.

Lincoln always knew what his commanding general was doing, through Halleck, Stanton, and his own regular visits to the telegraph office. He also visited Grant several times. Lincoln may have told Grant that he did not want to know the general's plans, but because the two men agreed on strategy, he knew well enough what these plans were. And he knew that Grant did not need the constant pressure he had had to apply to his earlier generals, so he left him alone.

Abraham Lincoln was not a perfect war leader, and he made mistakes. Unlike his Confederate counterpart, Jefferson Davis, he did not have the credentials of a military general. But also unlike

Davis, Lincoln was willing to learn, grow, and develop. The winner in war is the individual who approaches the inevitable chaos of the battlefield and the politics of the nation's capital with determination and an open mind. Lincoln did that, continuing to learn and learning well, and he became a successful wartime president as a result. And thus the Union was preserved and, to use words from Lincoln's Gettysburg Address, "this nation, under God," had "a new birth of freedom."

NOTES

INDEX

NOTES

1. "No Commander Ever Started with a Heavier Handicap"

1. U.S. Constitution, Article II, Sections 1, 2; Warren W. Hassler Jr., *The President as Commander in Chief* (Menlo Park, CA: Addison Wesley, 1971), 7.
2. Hassler, *President as Commander in Chief*, 10–14.
3. U.S. Constitution, Article I, Section 8. An excellent study of Lincoln's attitude and actions toward the Constitution is Daniel Farber, *Lincoln's Constitution* (Chicago: University of Chicago Press, 2003).
4. Hassler, *President as Commander in Chief*, 56.
5. Mackubin Thomas Owens, *Abraham Lincoln: Leadership and Democratic Statesmanship in Wartime* (Philadelphia: Foreign Policy Research Institute, 2009), 36.
6. Ibid., 8.
7. William Henry Herndon and Jesse W. Weik, *Herndon's Life of Lincoln* (New York: Albert and Charles Boni, 1936), 77–79; Hassler, *President as Commander in Chief*, 58; Trevor Nevitt Dupuy, *The Military Life of Abraham Lincoln, Commander in Chief* (New York: Franklin Watts, 1969), 5–6.
8. Herndon and Weik, *Life of Lincoln*, 79.
9. Abraham Lincoln, "Speech in U.S. House of Representatives on the Presidential Question," July 27, 1848, in *The Collected Works of Abraham Lincoln*, ed. Roy P. Basler (New Brunswick, NJ: Rutgers University Press, 1953), 1:509–10. Hereafter cited as *CW*.
10. Marvin R. Cain, "Lincoln as Soldier of the Union: A Reappraisal," *Lincoln Herald* 83 (Spring 1981): 593; Lincoln, "To Jesse W. Fell, Enclosing Autobiography," December 20, 1859, *CW* 3:512; similar statement in "Autobiography Written for John L. Scripps," c. June 1860, *CW* 4:62. An excellent brief account of Lincoln's military service in the Black Hawk War, emphasizing its impact on him as a Civil War military leader, is William C. Davis, *Lincoln's Men* (New York: Free Press, 1999).
11. Dale Thomas, "Lincoln and the Black Hawk War," Cleveland Civil War Roundtable *Charger* 26, no. 1 (2004).
12. February 28, 1840, *CW* 1:203–5.
13. December 22, 1847, *CW* 1:420–22.
14. February 1, May 21, 1848, *CW* 1:446–48, 472–73.
15. [March ? 1848], *CW* 1:454.
16. July 27, 1848, *CW* 1:501–16; Norma Lois Patterson, *Presidencies of William Henry Harrison and John Tyler*, American Presidency Series (Lawrence: University Press of Kansas, 1999).

17. Jefferson Davis to Winfield Scott, May 27, 1856, Appendix, January 31, 1856, in *The Papers of Jefferson Davis*, ed. Lynda L. Crist and Mary S. Dix (Baton Rouge: Louisiana State University Press, 1989), 6:25, 409.
18. June 25, October 5, 1858, November 3, 1860, *CW* 2:473–74, 3:206, Supp. 1:59; Allen Guelzo, *Lincoln and Douglas: The Debate That Defined America* (New York: Simon and Schuster, 1989).
19. Carl von Clausewitz, *On War* (New York: 1943), 248; Colin R. Ballard, *The Military Genius of Abraham Lincoln* (Cleveland: World Publishing Company, 1965), 3.

2. "Why Don't They Come!"

1. January 3, February 11, 22, 1861, *CW* 4:170, 194–96, 241. The best account of Lincoln's activities between his election and inauguration is Harold Holzer, *Lincoln President-Elect: Abraham Lincoln and the Great Secession Winter* (New York: Simon and Schuster, 2008).
2. John F. Marszalek, "Where Did Winfield Scott Find His Anaconda?," *Lincoln Herald*, 89 (Summer 1987): 77–81.
3. October 29, 1860, *CW* 4:137.
4. December 21, 1860, *CW* 4:157, 159.
5. Michael Burlingame, ed., *At Lincoln's Side: John Hay's Civil War and Selected Writings* (Carbondale: Southern Illinois University Press, 2000), xv; Thomas A. Horrocks, *President James Buchanan and the Crisis of National Leadership* (New York: Nova, 2012).
6. Doris Kearns Goodwin, *Team of Rivals: The Political Genius of Abraham Lincoln* (New York: Simon and Schuster, 2005).
7. Craig L. Symonds, "Lincoln, the Navy, and the Fort Sumter Crisis," *North and South Magazine* 11 (July 2009): 34–46.
8. March 9, 11, 15, 1861, *CW* 4:279, 284–85.
9. March 26, April 1, 1861, *CW* 4:299, 316–18.
10. April 6, 1861, *CW* 4:323–24; Symonds, "Lincoln, the Navy, and the Fort Sumter Crisis," 34–46.
11. Grady McWhiney, "The Confederacy's First Shot," *Civil War History* 14 (March 1968), 14.
12. April 15, 19, 1861, *CW* 4:331–32, 338–39.
13. April 23, 1861, Harold Holzer, ed., *Lincoln on War* (Chapel Hill, NC: Algonquin Books of Chapel Hill, 2011), 115; April 21, 1861, Michael Burlingame and John R. Turner Ettlinger, eds., *Inside Lincoln's White House: The Complete Civil War Diary of John Hay* (Carbondale: Southern Illinois University Press, 1997), 5. An early account of the riot, written by the 1861 mayor of Baltimore, is George William Brown, *Baltimore and the Nineteenth of April 1861: A Study of the War* (Baltimore: Johns Hopkins University, 1887).

14. April 22, 1861, *CW* 4:341–42.
15. April 27, May 3, 1861, *CW* 4:346–47, 353–54.
16. May 7, 13, 1861, *CW* 4:359, 367–68.
17. David Work, *Lincoln's Political Generals* (Urbana: University of Illinois Press, 2009).
18. May 24, 25, 1861, *CW* 4:385.
19. John V. Quarstein, *Big Bethel: The First Battle* (Charleston, SC: History Press, 2011).
20. June 17, 20, July 2, 1861, *CW* 4:409, 414, 419. See Nicole Etcheson, "James Henry Lane," in *Encyclopedia of the American Civil War*, ed. David S. Heidler and Jeanne T. Heidler (New York: Norton, 2000), 1141–42.
21. John F. Marszalek, "Lincoln's Special Session," *Civil War Times Illustrated* 10 (June 1971): 22–29.
22. James M. Lundberg, "On to Richmond! Or Not," *New York Times* Opinionator, July 28, 2011.
23. William C. Davis, *Battle at Bull Run* (New York: Doubleday, 1977).
24. July 23, 1861, *CW* 4:457.
25. July 27, 1861, *CW* 4:457–58.

3. "The Integrity of the Union [Is] Prominent"

1. July 23, 1861, *CW* 4:458; William T. Sherman, *Memoirs of General William T. Sherman*, 2 vols. (New York: New American Library, 1990), 1:206–8.
2. July 25, 27, 29, 30, August 1, 2, 7, 1861 *CW* 4:460, Supp. 1:86, 4:463, 8:593, Supp. 2:30, 4:468–69, 515; John Y. Simon, ed., *The Papers of Ulysses S. Grant*, 32 vols. (Carbondale: Southern Illinois University Press, 1967–2012), 3:88, 4:89, 4:482–83.
3. September 2, 9, 1861, *CW* 4:506–7, 513. The definitive book on John C. Fremont is Allan Nevins, *Fremont: The West's Greatest Adventurer*, 2 vols. (New York: Harper and Brothers, 1928).
4. September 12, 22, 1861, *CW* 4:519–20, 531–33.
5. John F. Marszalek, *Sherman: A Soldier's Passion for Order* (New York: Free Press, 1993), 141, 154–55.
6. October 1, 1861, *CW* 4:544–45.
7. October 7, 24 (two letters), 1861, *CW* 4:549–50, 562–63, 5:1–2.
8. November 1, 1861, Burlingame and Ettlinger, *Inside Lincoln's White House*, 30; Stephen B. Sears, *George B. McClellan: The Young Napoleon* (New York: Ticknor and Fields, 1988).
9. [c. October 11, 1861], Stephen W. Sears, ed., *The Civil War Papers of George B. McClellan: Selected Correspondence, 1860–1865* (New York: Ticknor and Fields, 1989), 106; November 13, 1861, Burlingame and Ettlinger, *Inside Lincoln's White House*, 30, 32.

10. [c. December 1], December 10, 1861, *CW* 5:334–35.
11. December 3, 1861, *CW* 5:37–53.
12. December 31, 1861, January 1, 1862 *CW* 5:84, 84n; Stephen D. Engle, *Don Carlos Buell: Most Promising of All* (Chapel Hill: University of North Carolina Press, 1999).
13. January 1, 7, 1862, *CW* 5:87, 92; January 10, 1862, Holzer, *Lincoln on War*, 147. Typhoid fever is a bacterial disease whose symptoms include high fever, headache, fatigue, diarrhea or constipation, and weight loss.
14. January 11, 1862, *CW* 5:96–97; Bruce Tap, *Over Lincoln's Shoulder: The Committee on the Conduct of the War* (Lawrence: University Press of Kansas, 1998); Benjamin P. Thomas and Harold M. Hyman, *Stanton: The Life and Times of Lincoln's Secretary of War* (New York: Knopf, 1962).
15. January 13, 27, 1862, *CW* 5:98–99, 111–12.
16. Helen Nicolay, *Lincoln's Secretary* (New York: Longmans Green, 1949), 132–33; Jean Edward Smith, *Grant* (New York: Simon and Schuster, 2002); Charles A. Roland, *Albert Sidney Johnston, Soldier of Three Republics* (Lexington: University Press in Kentucky, 2001).
17. See Simon, *Grant Papers*, 4:416n; and John F. Marszalek, *Commander of All Lincoln's Armies: A Life of General Henry W. Halleck* (Cambridge, MA: Belknap Press of Harvard University Press, 2004), 116–20.
18. Marszalek, *Commander of All Lincoln's Armies*, 117; April 3, 1862, *CW* 5:179.
19. March 6, 1862, *CW* 5:144–46; Ira Berlin, Joseph P. Reidy, and Leslie S. Rowland, eds., *Freedom's Soldiers: The Black Military Experience in the Civil War* (Cambridge, MA: Cambridge University Press, 1998), 3–5.
20. April 23, 1862, Simon, *Grant Papers*, 5:51n. There are several excellent books on the Battle of Shiloh. The most recent is Timothy B. Smith, *Shiloh: Conquer or Perish* (Lawrence: University Press of Kansas, 2014).
21. April 24, 1862, Simon, *Grant Papers*, 5:51n.
22. May 19, 1862, *CW* 5:222–24; Edward A. Miller Jr., *Lincoln's Abolitionist General: The Biography of David Hunter* (Columbia: University of South Carolina Press, 1995).
23. April 9, 1862, *CW* 5:184.
24. James M. McPherson, *Tried by War: Abraham Lincoln as Commander in Chief* (New York: Penguin Press, 2008), 89–90.
25. June 24, 1862, *CW* 5:284; June 24, 1862, Holzer, 16; June 28, 1862, *CW* 5:291–92, 296–97.
26. June 30, July 1, 1862, *CW* 5:293, 296.
27. July 2 (two letters), 1862, *CW* 5:300–301.
28. July 6, 8–9, 1862, *CW* 5:308, 309–12.

4. "Without Slavery the Rebellion Could Never Have Existed"

1. The modern biography of Henry W. Halleck is Marszalek, *Commander of All Lincoln's Armies.*
2. September 10, 1862, Gideon Welles, *Diary of Gideon Welles*, 3 vols. (Boston: Houghton Mifflin, 1911), 1:119–20.
3. Marszalek, *Halleck*, 129–54.
4. John J. Hennessy, *Return to Bull Run. The Campaign and Battle of Second* Manassas (Norman: University of Oklahoma Press, 1999); September 2, 1862, Welles, *Diary* 1:104–05; September 9, 1862, Chicago *Tribune,* cited in McPherson, *Tried by War*, 122.
5. James M. McPherson, *Crossroads of Freedom: Antietam* (New York: Oxford University Press, 2002).
6. July 17, 1862, *CW* 5:328–31; *The Statutes at Large, Treaties and Proclamations of the United States of America from December 5, 1859 to March 3, 1863*, ed. George P. Sanger (Boston: Little, Brown and Company, 1863), 589–92.
7. July 22, 1862, *CW* 5:338.
8. July 25, 1862, *CW* 5:341–42.
9. July 31, 1862, *CW* 5:350–51.
10. August 4, 1862, *CW* 5:356–57.
11. August 20, 22, 1862, *CW* 5:388–89.
12. September 13, 1862, Holzer, *Lincoln on War*, 176–78.
13. Harold Holzer, Edna Greene Medford, and Frank J. Williams, *The Emancipation Proclamation: Three Views* (Baton Rouge: Louisiana State University Press, 2006); September 26, 1862, *CW* 5:433–36
14. September 24, 1862, Holzer, *Lincoln on War*, 182.
15. October 13, 1862, *CW* 5:460–62.
16. October 24[25], 27, 1862, *CW* 5:474–75, 479.
17. Timothy B. Smith, *Corinth 1862: Siege, Battle, Occupation* (Lawrence: University Press of Kansas, 2012); October 8, 20, 1862, *CW* 5:453, 468–69.
18. September 2, [November 5], 1862, *CW* 5:486n.
19. November 5, 15, 1862, *CW* 5:485–86, 497–98.
20. Marszalek, *Commander of All Lincoln's Armies,* 156–57; November 27, 1862, *CW* 5:514–15.
21. December 1, 1862, *CW* 5:518–37.

5. "It Is the Old Difficulty"

1. December 22, 1862, *CW* 6:13. See George C. Rable, *Fredericksburg! Fredericksburg!* (Chapel Hill: University of North Carolina Press, 2002).
2. December 22, 1862, *CW* 6:15–16.
3. January 1, 1863, *CW* 6:31.

4. Marszalek, *Commander of All Lincoln's Armies*, 164–65.
5. There are a number of excellent books on the Emancipation Proclamation, starting with John Hope Franklin's longtime standard, *Reconstruction after the Civil War* (Chicago: University of Chicago Press, 1994). A recent book that not only presents factual information about the proclamation but also provides the insights of three Lincoln scholars is Holzer, Medford, and Williams, *Emancipation Proclamation*.
6. January 14, 15, 1863, *CW* 6:56.
7. March 26, 1862, *CW* 6:149–50.
8. April 1, 1862, *CW* 6:158.
9. Marszalek, *Commander of All Lincoln's Armies*, 165–66.
10. January 26, 1863, *CW* 6:78–79. The Hooker quote is in Noah Brooks, *Washington in Lincoln's Time* (New York: Century, 1895), 53.
11. Marszalek, *Commander of All Lincoln's Armies*, 160; January 5, 1863, *CW* 6:39.
12. March 16, 17, 1863, *CW* 6:138–40.
13. Sherman, *Memoirs*, 1:285; February 1, 1863, Simon, *Grant Papers*, 7:274.
14. January 7, 22, 1863, *CW* 6:70–71; Richard L. Kiper, *Major General John Alexander McClernand: Politician in Uniform* (Kent, OH: Kent State University Press, 1999).
15. An excellent collection of correspondence on this order is found in Simon, *Grant Papers*, 7:50n–56n; January 7, 21, 22, 1863, *CW*, 6:70–71. See also Jonathan D. Sarna, *When General Grant Expelled the Jews* (New York: Schocken, 2012).
16. [January 23?], 1863, *CW* 6:73–74.
17. January 25, 1863, Simon, *Grant Papers*, 7:252n. The definitive book on the Vicksburg Campaign is Michael B. Ballard, *Vicksburg: The Campaign That Opened the Mississippi* (Chapel Hill: University of North Carolina Press, 2004).
18. Marszalek, *Commander of All Lincoln's Armies*, 171; Gary W. Gallagher, ed., *Chancellorsville: The Battle and Its Aftermath* (Chapel Hill: University of North Carolina Press, 1996).
19. May 4, 6, 1863, Welles, *Diary*, 1:291, 293; May 7, 1863, *CW* 6:201.
20. May 14, 1863, *CW* 6:217.
21. May 13, 1863, *CW* 6:217–18.
22. May 22, 23, 1863, *CW* 6:226; May 24, 1863, Simon, *Grant Papers*, 8:254–55.
23. Marszalek, *Commander of All Lincoln's Armies*, 171.
24. May 18, 26, 1863, *CW* 6:230–31.
25. May 26, June 8, 1863, *CW* 6:234–35, 253.
26. May 29 (two letters), 1863, *CW* 6:237.
27. June 2, 4, 1863, *CW* 6:247.
28. June 5, 10 (two letters), 1853, *CW* 6:249:50, 257–58.

29. Marszalek, *Commander of All Lincoln's Armies*, 173.
30. June 3, 15, 16, 1863 *CW* 6:281–82.
31. June 16 (two letters), 1863, *CW* 6:282; Marszalek, *Commander of All Lincoln's Armies*, 174.
32. Marszalek, *Commander of All Lincoln's Armies*, 175.
33. June 18, 1863, Simon, *Grant Papers*, 8:385n; July 31, 1863, Welles, *Diary*, 1:386.
34. July 7, 1863, Welles, *Diary*, 1:364; July 7, 1863, *CW*, 6:319.

6. "He Is Managing the War"

1. July 11, 1863, Burlingame and Ettlinger, *Inside Lincoln's White House*, 61; July 14, 1863, *CW* 6:328.
2. July 14 (four letters), 1863, *CW* 6:328, 327–28.
3. July 4, 6, 1863, *CW* 6:318, 328; July 14, 1863, Burlingame and Ettlinger, *Inside Lincoln's White House*, 62.
4. September 21, 1863, Welles, *Diary*, 1:439–40; July 15, 1863, Burlingame and Ettlinger, *Inside Lincoln's White House*, 63.
5. July 13, 1863, *CW* 6:326; February 4, 1887, Simon, *Grant Papers*, 8:323n. There is no corroboration for this quote, which appears only in Sherman's postwar recollection.
6. July 21, 30, 1863, *CW* 6:342, 357; August 7, 1863, Burlingame, *At Lincoln's Side*, 49.
7. James G. Hollandsworth, *Pretense of Glory: The Life of General Nathaniel Banks* (Baton Rouge: Louisiana State University Press, 2005); August 5, 1863, *CW* 6:364–65.
8. August 9, 23, 1863, *CW* 6:374–75.
9. August 14, 1863, Burlingame, *At Lincoln's Side*, 50–51.
10. August 26, 1863, *CW* 6:406–10.
11. Martin H. Blatt, Thomas J. Brown, and Donald Yacovone, eds., *Hope & Glory: Essays on the Legacy of the 54th Massachusetts* Regiment (Amherst: University of Massachusetts Press, 2009); September 11, 1863, *CW* 6:440–41.
12. Marszalek, *Commander of All Lincoln's Armies*, 185.
13. Ibid.
14. Two excellent studies of the Battles of Chickamauga and Chattanooga, both by Peter Cozzens, are *The Terrible Sound: The Battle of Chickamauga* (Urbana: University of Illinois Press, 1992) and *Shipwreck of Their Hopes: The Battles for Chattanooga* (Urbana: University of Illinois Press, 1994).
15. September 27, 1863, Burlingame and Ettlinger, *Inside Lincoln's White House*, 85.
16. September 21 (two letters), 22, 1863, *CW* 6:470–75.

17. Marszalek, *Commander of All Lincoln's Armies*, 187.
18. Marszalek, *Sherman*, 240.
19. December 8, 1863, Simon, *Grant Papers*, 9:503.
20. September 15, 1863, *CW* 6:450.
21. September 19, 1863, *CW* 6:466–68.
22. October 3, 5, 1863, *CW* 6:492–93, 499–504; William E. Parrish, *Turbulent Partnership: Missouri and the Union, 1861–1865* (Columbia: University of Missouri Press, 1963).
23. October 17, 1863, *CW* 6:523–24.
24. [November 2, 1863], *CW* 6:559–61.
25. November 17, 1863, *CW* 7:16–17.
26. There are many excellent books about the Gettysburg Address. A particularly good one is Garry Wills, *Lincoln at Gettysburg: The Words That Made America* (New York: Simon and Schuster, 1992).
27. December 8, 1863, *CW* 7:53–56.
28. December 20, 1863, *CW* Supp. 1:84.
29. [January 1864?], *CW* 7:101–102; Holzer, *Lincoln on War*, 255, and December 8, 1863, 250–53. Some historians have questioned the legitimacy of the Wadsworth letter. Holzer's inclusion of it in his book is a good argument for its validity, but Daniel W. Stowell, the director of *The Papers of Abraham Lincoln* project, believes that "more research must be done." Stowell, e-mail message to author, July 16, 2013. A short study of Lorenzo Thomas is Michael A. Eggleston, *President Lincoln's Recruiter: General Lorenzo Thomas and the United States Colored Troops* (Jefferson, NC: McFarland, 2013).

7. "He Has the *Grit* of a Bulldog!"

1. January 6, 1864, *CW* Supp. 1:214–18. In 1883, a year after the Supreme Court decided that the 1864 action was unconstitutional, Robert E. Lee's son Custis sold the Arlington home and property to the United States. See *United States v. Lee*, 106 US 196.
2. January 5, 6, 8, 17, 1864, *CW* 7:109, 134–35.
3. January 23, February 1, 1864, *CW* 7:145–46, 164–65.
4. February 18, 1864, *CW* 7:191.
5. February 22, 1864, *CW* 7:200–201.
6. February 23, 29, 1864, *CW* 7:200, 212–13.
7. March 4, 7, 1864, *CW* 7:222–23.
8. Marszalek, *Commander of All Lincoln's Armies*, 194; February 29, 1864, *CW* Supp. 1: 226.
9. Marszalek, *Commander of All Lincoln's Armies*, 194,
10. March 24, 1864, Burlingame and Ettlinger, *Inside Lincoln's White House*, 183; Marszalek, *Commander of All Lincoln's Armies*, 197–99.

11. See Frederick Maurice, "Lincoln as a Strategist," *The Forum* 75 (February 1926): 164 for an early statement of the thesis that Lincoln did not give up control over the war. Cain, "Lincoln as Soldier of the Union," 594; [March 9, 1864], *CW* 7:234–35.
12. [September 14?], 1863, March 14, 1864, *CW* 6:444–49, 7:245.
13. March 23, 1864, *CW* 7:262.
14. March 27, 1864, Burlingame and Ettlinger, *Inside Lincoln's White House*, 187; March 15, 29, 1864, *CW* 7:273–74.
15. March 31, 1864, *CW* 7:276.
16. Many books and articles have been written on the massacre at Fort Pillow. A good account of the facts and their interpretation is John Cimprich, *Fort Pillow: A Civil War Massacre and Public Memory* (Baton Rouge: Louisiana State University Press, 2005).
17. April 18, 1864, *CW* 7:301–3.
18. May 3, 17, 1864, *CW* 7:328–29, 345–46.
19. May 19, 1864, *CW* Supp. 1:243–44.
20. Marszalek, *Sherman*, 257–63.
21. April 30, 1864, *CW* 7:324.
22. May 1, 1864, Simon, *Grant Papers*, 10:380; May 1864, Francis B. Carpenter, *The Inner Life of Abraham Lincoln: Six Months at the White House* (New York: Hurd and Houghton, 1867), 283.
23. May 4, 5, 1864, *CW* 7:330–31.
24. April 30, 1864, Burlingame and Ettlinger, *Inside Lincoln's White House*, 194.
25. May 7, 9, 1864, *CW* 7:332–34.
26. May 18 (two letters), 19, 1864, *CW* 7:347–50.
27. June 9, 1864, *CW* 7:380–82.
28. June 13, 1864, *CW* 7:390.
29. June 24, July 14, 1864, *CW* 7: 404–6.
30. June 15 (two letters), 1864, *CW* 7:393; William O. Stoddard, *Inside the White House in War Times: Memoir and Reports of Lincoln's Secretary*, ed. Michael Burlingame (Lincoln: University of Nebraska Press, 2000), 126.
31. June 16, 1864, *CW* 7:393–96.
32. June 24, 1864, *CW* 7:406; June 23, 1864, Burlingame and Ettlinger, *Inside Lincoln's White House*, 210.
33. July 1, 1864, Simon, *Grant Papers*, 11:125–26.
34. July 10, 1864, *CW* 7:437.
35. Frank E. Vandiver, *Jubal's Raid: General Early's Famous Attack on Washington in 1864* (Lincoln: University of Nebraska Press, 1992). According to James M. McPherson, "There is no definitive evidence for or against the story that Holmes was the man who ordered Lincoln to get down." McPherson, *Tried by War*, 22.

36. The best book on these riots is Iver Bernstein, *The New York City Draft Riots: Their Significance for American Society and Politics in the Age of the Civil War* (New York: Oxford University Press, 1990).

8. "A Victory Worth More . . . Than a Battle Won"

1. July 18, 1864, *CW* 7:451.
2. July 25, 1864, *CW* 7:459–61.
3. August 17, 1864, *CW* 7:499–502; John G. Nicolay and John Hay, *Abraham Lincoln: A History*, 10 vols. (New York: Century, 1890), 9:184–200.
4. July 26, 1864, Simon, *Grant Papers*, 11:315–16; August 3, 4, 1864, *CW* 7:476–77.
5. August 17, 1864, *CW* 7:499.
6. August 18, 31, 1864, *CW* 7:504–5, 528–29.
7. August 19, 1864, *CW* 7:506–8.
8. August 22, 1864, *CW* 7:514–15.
9. August 23, 1864, *CW* 7:514.
10. August 24, 1864, *CW* 7:517–18; Nicolay and Hay, *Abraham Lincoln*, 9:184–200.
11. September 3, 1864, *CW* 7:532–34.
12. September 10, [c. September 12], 1864, *CW* 7:548–50.
13. [c. September 7, 1864], CW 7:539; September 9, 21, 1864, Simon, *Grant Papers*, 12:138, 185.
14. September 12, 1864, *CW* 8:1–2.
15. September 19, 1864, *CW* 8:11.
16. September 29, 1864, *CW* 8:29; September 29, 1864, Simon, *Grant Papers*, 12:228–29; September 29, 1864, Burlingame and Ettlinger, *Inside Lincoln's White House*, 234.
17. Marszalek, *Sherman*, 292–95.
18. October 12, 1864, Simon, *Grant Papers*, 12:303n; Marszalek, *Sherman*, 295.
19. Earl J. Hess, *Into the Crater: The Mine Attack at Petersburg* (Columbia: University of South Carolina, 1993).
20. October 22, 1864, *CW* 8:73–74.
21. April 28, 1864, Welles, *Diary*, 1:287; December 17, 18, 1864, Simon, *Grant Papers*, 13:128n–29n. Amanda Foreman, *A World on Fire: Britain's Crucial Role in the American Civil War* (New York: Random House, 2010).
22. November 10, 1864 (two letters), *CW* 8:100; Simon, *Grant Papers*, 12:398; David E. Long, *The Jewel of Liberty: Abraham Lincoln's Re-election and the End of Slavery* (Mechanicsburg, PA: Stackpole Books, 1994).
23. Marszalek, *Sherman*, 306–9.
24. Marszalek, *Commander of All Lincoln's Armies*, 217.
25. December 6, 16, 1864, *CW* 8:154, 169.

26. December 26, 1864, *CW* 8:181–82.
27. December 6, 1864, *CW* 8:136–53.

9. "He Will Stand in History beside Washington, Perhaps Higher"

1. Marszalek, *Sherman*, 306–18.
2. January 4, 6, 7, 1865, Simon, *Grant Papers*, 13:223.
3. December 31, 1864, *CW* 8:201.
4. January 5, 1865, *CW* 8:201.
5. January 19, 1865, *CW* 8:223.
6. January, 21, 22, Simon, *Grant Papers*, 13:281, 282; Jason Emerson, *Giant in the Shadows: The Life of Robert T. Lincoln* (Carbondale: Southern Illinois University Press, 2012).
7. January 18, February 10, 1865, *CW* 8:220–21, 274–85.
8. February 10, 1865, *CW* 8:274–85.
9. January 30, 31, 1865, *CW* 8:246, 250–51.
10. February 1, 1865, *CW* 8:252; February 1, 1865, Simon, *Grant Papers*, 13:344–45.
11. February 6, 1865, Welles, *Diary*, 2:237.
12. February 8, 10, 1865, *CW* 8:269, 274–85; February 2, 1865, Welles, *Diary*, 2:235; William C. Harris, "The Hampton Roads Peace Conference: A Final Test of Lincoln's Presidential Leadership," *Journal of the Abraham Lincoln Association* 21 (January 2000): 30–61.
13. March 3, 1865, *CW* 8:330–331.
14. February 6, 7, [7?], 1865, *CW* 8:264–65, 266, 268; January 6, 1865, Welles, *Diary*, 2:222. Many writings insist that there were huge numbers of black Confederate soldiers. See, for example, the Black Confederate Warriors of Dixie, at www.blackconfederates.blogspot.com (accessed October 12, 2013). An excellent, accurate study that demonstrates the invalidity of such a belief is Bruce Levine, *Confederate Emancipation: Southern Plans to Free and Arm Slaves during the Civil War* (New York: Oxford University Press, 2007).
15. March 2, 1865 (two letters), Simon, *Grant Papers*, 14: 80–81; March 3, 1865, *CW* 8:331.
16. March 4, 1865, Welles, *Diary*, 2:252; March 4, 1865, *CW* 8:332–33; Ronald C. White Jr., *Lincoln's Greatest Speech: The Second Inaugural* (New York: Simon and Schuster, 2002); Frederick Douglass, *The Complete Autobiographies of Frederick Douglass*, ed. Henry Louis Gates (New York: Library of America, 1994), 482. For an excellent brief analysis of this speech, see Ronald C. White, *The Eloquent President: A Portrait of Lincoln through His Words* (New York: Random House, 2005), 277–301.
17. March 20, 1865, *CW* 8:367.

18. Ibid.; March 29, 1865, Simon, *Grant Papers*, 14:248; March 25, 1865, *CW* 8:374.
19. Marszalek, *Sherman*, 336–37.
20. March 30, 31, 1865, *CW* 8:377–78.
21. April 2 (three letters), 3, 1865, *CW* 8:381–85.
22. April 2, 7, 1865, *CW* 8:383, 392.
23. April 6 (two letters), 1865, *CW* 8:388–89; "Lincoln's Visit to Richmond," National Park Service, accessed October 12, 2013, www.nps.gov/rich/historyculture/lincvisit.htm.
24. April 11, 1865, *CW* 8:399–405.
25. April 14, 1865, Holzer, *Lincoln on War*, 317; May 14, 1865, George Templeton Strong, *The Diary of George Templeton Strong: The Civil War, 1860–1865*, ed. Allan Nevins and Milton Halsey Thomas (New York: Macmillan, 1952), 597–98.

INDEX

Images are indicated by the letter *G* before the number of the page on which each appears within the gallery.

John F. Marszalek is the Giles Distinguished Professor Emeritus of History at Mississippi State University and the executive director and managing editor of the Ulysses S. Grant Association's Grant Presidential Library at Mississippi State University. He is the award-winning author or editor of fourteen books, including biographies of William T. Sherman and Henry W. Halleck, and books and articles on Jacksonian America and race relations.

CONCISE
LINCOLN
LIBRARY

This series of concise books fills a need for short studies of the life, times, and legacy of President Abraham Lincoln. Each book gives readers the opportunity to quickly achieve basic knowledge of a Lincoln-related topic. These books bring fresh perspectives to well-known topics, investigate previously overlooked subjects, and explore in greater depth topics that have not yet received book-length treatment. For a complete list of current and forthcoming titles, see www.conciselincolnlibrary.com.

Other Books in the Concise Lincoln Library

Abraham Lincoln and Horace Greeley
Gregory A. Borchard

Lincoln and the Civil War
Michael Burlingame

Lincoln and the Constitution
Brian R. Dirck

Lincoln and the Election of 1860
Michael S. Green

Lincoln and the Union Governors
William C. Harris

Lincoln's Campaign Biographies
Thomas A. Horrocks

Lincoln and Reconstruction
John C. Rodrigue

Lincoln and Medicine
Glenna R. Schroeder-Lein

Lincoln and the U.S. Colored Troops
John David Smith

Lincoln's Assassination
Edward Steers, Jr.

Lincoln and Race
Richard Striner

Lincoln and Religion
Ferenc Morton Szasz with Margaret Connell Szasz

Lincoln and the War's End
John C. Waugh

Lincoln as Hero
Frank J. Williams

Abraham and Mary Lincoln
Kenneth J. Winkle